COOKING WITH
FLAVOR BOMBS™

COOKING WITH
FLAVOR BOMBS™

PREP IT + FREEZE IT + DROP IT = TRANSFORM DINNER!

GIOVANNINA BELLINO

Race Point
PUBLISHING

Quarto is the authority on a wide range of topics.

Quarto educates, entertains and enriches the lives of our readers—enthusiasts and lovers of hands-on living.

www.quartoknows.com

First published in the United States of America in 2016 by
Race Point Publishing, a member of
Quarto Publishing Group USA Inc.
142 West 36th Street, 4th Floor
New York, NY 10018
www.quartoknows.com

10 9 8 7 6 5 4 3 2 1

ISBN: 978-1-63106-257-5

Library of Congress Cataloging-in-Publication Data

Names: Bellino, Giovannina, author.
Title: Cooking with flavor bombs prep it, freeze it, drop it...transform
  dinner! / Giovannina Bellino.
Description: New York : Race Point Publishing, 2017. | Includes index.
Identifiers: LCCN 2016031277 | ISBN 9781631062575 (hardcover)
Subjects: LCSH: Cooking (Herbs) | Cooking (Spices) | LCGFT: Cookbooks.
Classification: LCC TX819.H4 B3887 2017 | DDC 641.6/57--dc23 LC record available at
https://lccn.loc.gov/2016031277

Editorial Director: Jeannine Dillon
Project Editor: Erin Canning
Art Director: Merideth Harte
Photography: Evi Abeler
Photo Shoot Assistant: Harriet Honkaniemi
Food Stylist: Charlotte Omnès
Assistant Food Stylists: Eva Mrak Blumberg, Kristin Stangl, and Julia Choi

Printed in China

CONTENTS

iNTRODUCTiON

GARDENERS KNOW FLAVOR BOMBS. CHEFS KNOW FLAVOR BOMBS. AND NOW iT'S TiME FOR YOU TO KNOW FLAVOR BOMBS!

I've never been one to spend an entire day cooking meals for the week. The thought of that much shopping, prepping, cooking, and storing of meals is overwhelming to me. I mean, it would feel like holiday cooking every week. I do, however, spend an hour or two making a few batches of Flavor Bombs. The time spent on doing this sets my family up for quick and easy meals for the next month, if not two months. When I can eliminate the tedious chores of peeling, washing, chopping, and sautéing the herbs and aromatics for flavor bases every time I cook—now that's time well spent.

So if you find yourself grabbing the onion, garlic, carrots, celery, and any other veggies and fresh herbs to prep day after day, night after night, meal after meal, it's time to prep it, freeze it, and drop the "F Bomb."

Finally, if you enjoy cooking at all, it's such a great feeling of accomplishment when you start seeing (and tasting) your dishes reaching a new level of flavor. You will also begin using less salt and dried, packaged, or jarred spice mixes full of preservatives and start loving the full, deep flavors that YOU are creating.

—Giovannina Bellino

WHAT ARE FLAVOR BOMBS?

Flavor Bombs are combinations of savory, sautéed aromatics, fresh herbs, or sauce reductions blended together and frozen in ice cube trays, small containers, small bowls, or even just spooned onto a tray lined with wax paper. They are also a great way to reuse plastic containers, such as small sauce containers with lids and egg cartons. Once they're frozen, you transfer them to an airtight container or resealable freezer bag and they're ready to add a flavor explosion to your meals.

The ingredients are chopped by hand, in a food processor, or even pounded with a mortar and pestle, depending on how rustic or refined you want your Flavor Bomb blends to be. Fresh ingredients may be preferable but using pre-prepped, chopped vegetables in containers or even frozen vegetables will produce very similar results. The herbs, however, should always be fresh.

Making Flavor Bombs is an excellent way to take advantage of specials in your market's produce department. Stock up, chop up, and free up time and money! Go that extra mile when you buy that pricey batch of herbs or exotic vegetable, make enough for leftovers, and then make a Bomb out of it.

COMPONENTS OF A SUCCESSFUL FLAVOR BOMB

A successful flavor bomb includes the five basic tastes: sweetness, sourness, bitterness, saltiness, and umami. Along with the other ingredients in your dish, you may detect these flavors now more than ever since you are creating the background or building block of the dish with Flavor Bombs. By the way, spicy is not a taste, it hits the pain receptors, not the taste buds—so go as spicy as you dare!

SWEETNESS: Found in "sweet" vegetables, such as onions and carrots, sugars are drawn out when these vegetables are caramelized.

SOURNESS: Found in vinegar and lemon, sourness brings a brightness to the tongue, which contrasts nicely with rich, savory flavors and can help cut through fattiness.

BITTERNESS: Different than sourness, bitterness can be considered unpleasant but yet rounds out richness and adds another dimension of taste to dishes. It is found in citrus peel, herbs, and leafy greens.

SALTINESS: Identified with foods containing sodium, such as soy sauce, miso paste, and even celery, salt harmonizes and brings out the flavors of foods when used in moderation. It shares some characteristics with umami.

UMAMI: This Japanese word means "yummy" or "delicious" (and it is). Umami has a meaty, savory taste that is found in miso paste, soy sauce, tomato paste, and dried mushrooms.

TYPES OF FLAVOR BOMBS

I have included three types of Flavor Bombs in this book—Herb Pesto, Vegetable Blend, and Stock and Sauce—that represent flavors from around the world. I have also included recipes with all of the Bombs to get you started, but feel free to experiment with your own blends.

HERB PESTO FLAVOR BOMBS

The word "pesto" derives from the Italian verb *pestare*, which means to pound the ingredients in a mortar and pestle to create a "paste." In this section, you'll find your classic Italian basil pesto to Mediterranean, Thai, Tex-Mex, and Latin American versions. What do all of the pestos have in common? Fresh herbs, sautéed aromatics, and extra-virgin olive oil. Some of them call for the addition of flat leaf (Italian) parsley, which gives a bright green color and rounds out the flavor.

Pesto recipes can be easily customized to your own tastes. If nut or cheese sensitivity is an issue, just eliminate them. You can make your pesto denser, looser, greener, nuttier, or with extra garlic. Here are some basic cooking uses for Herb Pesto Flavor Bombs:

- As a marinade or salad dressing thinned with oil or broth
- As a rub or crust for roasting
- In stuffing and bread crumbs
- In ravioli or other stuffed pasta filling
- For herb butters, dipping oils, or dips
- As a braising base for stovetop cooking
- In slow cooker recipes
- In omelets, batters, and quiche
- As a bruschetta topping
- As a sandwich spread blended with mayo, mustard, or oil

You may also want to give these pesto combinations a try:
- Gremolata (lemon zest, garlic, and parsley)
- Arugula, garlic, and walnuts
- Swiss chard, garlic, and pignoli
- Broccoli rabe, garlic, and raisins
- Olives, red peppers, and parsley or basil
- Mint, peas, and shallots
- Creamed spinach pesto

Here is the quickest and easiest method for making multiple Herb Pesto Flavor Bombs at the same time. See the Herb Pesto Flavor Bomb recipes for specific ingredients and more detailed instruction once you have your ingredients prepped.

TOAST THE NUTS
Lightly toast the nuts, one type at a time, in a dry large sauté pan over medium heat for 2 to 3 minutes. Remove from the pan and set aside in separate bowls.

SAUTÉ THE AROMATICS
Peel and roughly chop the garlic (at least 3 bulbs), shallot (about 5 bulbs), and onion (about 4 bulbs), keeping them separate. Add extra-virgin olive oil to the same large sauté pan that the nuts were toasted in, then lightly sauté each aromatic, separately, until fragrant. Remove from the pan and set aside in separate bowls.

STEM AND WASH THE HERBS
Parsley, sage, cilantro, and basil: Cut as much of the stems off the bunch as possible and then pick the leaves off into a large bowl. Swish the leaves around in cold water, let sit for a couple of minutes for grit to fall to the bottom of the bowl, and then scoop into a colander and repeat. Shake in the colander, use a salad spinner, or lay on paper towels to dry—the herbs don't have to be totally dry, just not dripping wet. **Rosemary and oregano:** Hold the "branch" in one hand, using the other hand to "strip" it in the opposite direction of the leaf growth. Because oregano is more delicate, you will also have to pick off leaves from the "branch." Wash and dry using the same method as for parsley, sage, cilantro, and basil, but use a mesh strainer instead of a colander, so you don't lose the needle-like leaves down the drain.

A good size bunch of parsley, cilantro, or sage will yield approximately 3 cups (120 to 180 g) of leaves per bunch; basil will yield approximately 2 cups (80 g) of leaves per bunch; and rosemary or oregano will yield approximately 1½ cups (40 g) of leaves per bunch (rosemary is pungent so even a cup may be sufficient for your recipe).

VEGETABLE-BLEND FLAVOR BOMBS

Soffritto, sofrito, mirepoix, holy trinity, suppengrün . . . these international terms all basically mean the same thing: a blend of sautéed vegetables used as flavor bases. The word *soffritto* roughly translates to "slowly fry" in Italian; the Spanish version, *sofrito*, always contains tomatoes.

Most cuisines have a traditional combination of aromatics. Aromatics are herbs, spices, and vegetables, such as onions, garlic, and shallots, that are cooked in oil as a base for the flavor of a dish. Cooking them in butter and/or oil helps to release their flavors and aromas, creating a deep flavor foundation for soups, stews, sauces, meat fillings, and more.

In French cooking, the combination is the classic *mirepoix*, which is called the "holy trinity" in Creole/Cajun cuisine. Both are a blend of onions and celery with either carrots (French) or green peppers (Cajun) that are sautéed in butter and/or oil, and are the base of so many dishes. Mirepoix mixes perfectly in any grain as a side dish or stuffing, tosses with any vegetable to give it extra flavor and color, or mixes into a tuna, chicken, or other salad for a savory burst of flavor. Meanwhile, German cooks use *suppengrün*, which typically consists of carrots, celery root, and leeks.

I have also included an Indian Curry Flavor Bomb and an Umami Flavor Bomb in this section to bring in some Asian flavors.

Here are some basic cooking uses for Vegetable-Blend Flavor Bombs:

- To mix into any grain or pasta for a side dish
- To mix into a homemade stuffing
- To give any vegetable extra flavor and color
- To mix into a tuna, chicken, or other salad for a savory burst of flavor
- As a base for soups, stews, and slow-cooked dishes
- In stir-fry dishes, omelets, quiche, and sandwiches and panini

STOCK AND SAUCE FLAVOR BOMBS

In this section, I have included just a few of the many basic components of cooking that a chef learns to master: a béchamel sauce (or white sauce) and beef, chicken, and vegetable stocks. A home cook should know how to make these essentials, too. I believe that if you can make a great sauce, then more than half the battle is won in that fight to get a delicious meal onto the table.

Today it is often called a "bone broth," but it is really just a stock. Don't let the long cooking times of the Stock Flavor Bombs scare you. One of the easiest things to make is a stock. It can simmer at a low temperature while you go about your day and give it the occasional stir—you can even run a quick errand or take a walk. Some recipes say to leave it simmering overnight, but I have to admit that I'm hesitant to do that. I'd rather start at the crack of dawn and put it to rest when I do.

If you reduce a stock even longer, by half, it becomes a *demi glace*. The concept behind the Stock Flavor Bombs is to have units of stock on hand to make a demi glace, and then the perfect pan sauce, without having to use overly salty and fatty store-bought versions. If you buy a top-quality demi glace, it can be quite expensive, so making your own will also save money. The long cooking time brings out the gelatin in the bones; that's why it solidifies when it's chilled. Your sauces will have a great mouthfeel since it acts like a natural thickening agent.

Here are some basic cooking uses for Stock and Sauce Flavor Bombs:

- As a braising liquid
- As a base for pan sauces and gravies
- As a liquid to cook rice and grains
- As a soup base or just for sipping as a broth
- As a marinade, mixed with herbs and spices
- As a thickener (Bechamel Flavor Bomb)
- To add body to a soup or stew (stocks)

TOOLS OF THE TRADE

Along with the basic kitchen tools you most likely already have in your kitchen—saucepans, stock pots, cutting boards, knives, etc.—here are some additional tools and appliances that are helpful in making, freezing, and storing your homemade Flavor Bombs.

MAKING

FOOD PROCESSOR: a small or large one will come in handy, especially when making Herb Pesto Flavor Bombs. If you don't have a food processor, you can use a mortar and pestle, the original food processor—it's wonderful for making small amounts of aromatic "pastes" of a coarse consistency or for grinding spices.

KITCHEN SCALE (OPTIONAL): For a more serious cook, it's always good to own a kitchen scale for precision (and to become more familiar with weight measurements), especially when baking.

MEASURING SPOONS: This kitchen mainstay is essential for when you may want to increase or decrease the spice amounts in your Flavor Bombs to your taste.

MESH STRAINER: This is a must-have for straining the Stock Flavor Bombs.

STRAINER AND LARGE BOWL: These two items work hand in hand and are crucial for washing, rinsing, and drying herbs and vegetables, which are at the core of these Flavor Bombs.

FREEZING

ICE CUBE TRAYS: Standard ice cube trays have 14 cubes that are each 1 ounce (28 g). I also use some of the newer silicone trays that are 3 ounces (85 g) per cube and even ½ ounce (14 g) per cube.

PLASTIC EGG CARTONS: The indentations are usually 1 ounce (28 g) in size, just like a standard ice cube tray. An egg carton is perfect for oily or pungent Bombs so that you can just toss it out after using, without the hassle of soaking or washing to get rid of the scent.

PLASTIC TAKE-OUT CONTAINERS: Stockpile the small cups with lids (these usually hold soy sauce, ketchup, etc.) as they are 1 ounce (28 g) in size—the perfect size for a Flavor Bomb.

WAX PAPER: If the above options are unavailable to you, you can always spoon dollops of your mixtures onto this for freezing.

STORING

Once your Bombs are frozen, transfer them to either an airtight container or a resealable freezer bag for storage in your freezer for up to a year. Also, label your containers and bags!

HOW TO USE FLAVOR BOMBS

When following the Bomb recipes, a total ounce (gram) size is given for the yield. When following the dish recipes, the Bomb is listed in the ingredients list as, for example, 1 Sage Flavor Bomb or 4 Chicken Stock Bombs. Here's what you need to remember: **1 Bomb = 1 ounce (28 g)**. So if 4 Bombs are called for, that means 4 Bombs = 4 ounces (112 g). A nice little perk of making Flavor Bombs is that you get really savvy with knowing your measurements and can eyeball an ounce (28 g) or two (56 g) easily—this is a great cooking skill to develop!

Flavor Bombs are somewhat condensed, caramelized, or reduced blends of ingredients, so a little can go a long way. You can use your Flavor Bombs for the simplest preparation or in the most complex recipes. Here's how they work:

- A quick 30 seconds in the microwave will defrost your Bombs for blending with other ingredients, or dropped in a pot of soup, stew, or sauce while the Bomb is still frozen will do the trick!

- Dropping one in a dish that's just about finished yet needs "something" is one of the best ways to use them.

- Instead of salt and/or a fat, "drop a Bomb."

NO MORE WASTE!

Having ready-made elements in your freezer will make cooking future dishes a snap. It will also encourage you to start experimenting with mixing flavors. And why not have starters on hand to build a new dish re-created from a dish you already love? Once you are in the habit of preserving your excess produce and saving leftovers, you will develop a stockpile of essences in your freezer that will save you time and money (and the environment). You are basically creating your own Flavor Bombs! And remember to reuse your plastic containers for freezing your Bombs, such as those little sauce containers with lids and egg cartons.

EXCESS PRODUCE

I started making Flavor Bombs from the bounty of my vegetable garden, so if you get overzealous at the farmers' market, or have an abundant garden, all of that produce doesn't have to go to waste. Here are some useful tips:

- Wash, rinse, and dry herbs; mince in a food processor; lay on a baking sheet; and freeze. Use a spatula to transfer to container when frozen. Sprinkle in your cooking.

- Caramelize chopped onions, garlic, or shallots and then freeze.

- For sauce and stewed tomatoes, simmer overripe tomatoes for 45 minutes in salted water, let cool, squish by hand, reduce the liquid, and freeze. For homemade tomato paste, purée before freezing.

- Chop, wash, and freeze leeks (even the green parts), and then sauté with oil or butter to serve, or add to soups and stews.

- A cauliflower head goes a long way: chop and freeze; mince some (raw) in a food processor for "rice" without the carbs, freeze, and then steam to serve; or slice cauliflower "steaks," freeze, and then brush with oil, season, and grill to serve.

- Sauté mushrooms—mince some, slice some—and freeze.

- Save some herb stems, broccoli stalks, celery leaves, and carrot peels and simmer in water to make a quick veggie broth. Strain, and then freeze the broth in ice cube trays.

- Make a vegetable concentrate by using your food processor to turn your extra veggies into a paste. Combine them with soy sauce, tomato paste, and/or salt; freeze in ice cube trays or in dollops on wax paper; and add to your cooking for a flavor boost.

LEFTOVERS

Get in the habit of freezing bits of meals! What I mean by that is saving small amounts of that fabulous gravy on your meatloaf, skimming the chicken fat (schmaltz) from your soup, and reserving some of that bacon grease, rub, marinade, or herb blend. Saving small amounts of stuffing or vegetables will also provide you with a savory mixture to either purée for a sauce or reuse as a breading.

- Shrimp and lobster shells can be simmered with oil, a carrot, a celery stalk, and some parsley for lovely shellfish oil.

- Sauté shrimp and lobster shells in butter and simmer with water and vegetables for a stock. Strain into an ice cube tray.

- Never throw bread away. Tear it and toss it in the food processor for homemade bread crumbs. Season with grated Parmesan, herbs, salt, and pepper, or other flavor variations.

- Make a quick chicken broth using a rotisserie chicken's bones.

- Always spoon out and freeze some of your homemade tomato sauce. Use in meatballs and meatloaf or add it to brown pan sauces for depth of flavor.

SAGE
FLAVOR BOMB

ROSEMARY
FLAVOR BOMB

HERB PESTO
FLAVOR BOMBS

TEX-MEX
FLAVOR BOMB

BASIL
FLAVOR BOMB

CHIMICHURRI
FLAVOR BOMB

THAI
FLAVOR BOMB

BASIL FLAVOR BOMB

MAKES 14 OUNCES (392 G)

- ½ cup (68 g) pignoli (pine nuts)
- ½ to ¾ cup (120 to 180 ml) extra-virgin olive oil, divided
- ½ to ¾ cup (70 to 100 g) roughly chopped garlic
- 2 cups (40 g) basil, stemmed and packed
- 1 cup (60 g) flat leaf parsley, stemmed and packed
- ½ cup (50 g) grated Pecorino Romano
- Salt, to taste
- Pepper, to taste

1. Lightly toast the pignoli in a dry medium sauté pan over medium heat for 2 to 3 minutes. Remove from the pan and set aside.

2. Heat half the olive oil in the same pan, then lightly sauté the garlic over medium heat until fragrant, about 2 to 3 minutes. Remove from the pan and set aside.

3. Pulse the basil and parsley in a food processor to roughly chop, then add the cheese, pignoli, garlic, remaining olive oil, and salt and pepper to the food processor. Pulse again to the desired consistency. Do not purée.

4. Spoon the pesto into ice cube trays or small containers, or onto a wax paper–lined baking sheet or tray, and freeze. Once frozen, transfer the Flavor Bombs to an airtight container or a resealable freezer bag.

BASIL FLAVOR BOMB

SPAGHETTI FRITTATA SERVES 4 TO 6

> ½ box (½ pound/228 g) spaghetti, linguini, or capellini (or leftover cooked noodles, unsauced)
> 6 eggs
> 2 tablespoons (30 ml) half-and-half
> Salt, to taste
> Pepper, to taste
> 1 Basil Flavor Bomb
> ½ cup (50 g) grated Parmesan or Pecorino Romano cheese, divided
> ¼ cup (60 ml) extra-virgin olive oil, divided
> ½ cup (40 g) chopped pancetta, prosciutto, or dried sausage
> ¼ cup (34 g) pignoli (pine nuts)

1. Boil and drain the spaghetti and set aside.

2. In a bowl, beat the eggs with half-and-half, salt, and pepper, and then blend in the Basil Flavor Bomb and ¼ cup (25 g) grated cheese. Set aside.

3. In a large, nonstick, ovenproof frying pan, heat 2 tablespoons (30 ml) olive oil over medium heat and quickly sauté the pancetta and pignoli for a little golden color. Remove from the pan and set aside.

4. Preheat the oven to 350°F (180°C, or gas mark 4).

5. Add the remaining 2 tablespoons (30 ml) olive oil to the frying pan. Add the spaghetti to the pan, spreading it out. Let it sizzle for a minute or two to get a little color on the bottom.

6. Pour the egg mixture over the spaghetti, using a spatula to make sure it completely covers it and gets in between and underneath the spaghetti. Let the eggs cook, rotating the pan and using the spatula to lift edges, letting the uncooked egg underneath cook (as if making an omelet).

7. When the eggs are set, sprinkle the pancetta, pignoli, and remaining ¼ cup (25 g) grated cheese on the top, spreading it around to evenly distribute. Put the pan in the oven and let the frittata bake until the eggs are cooked and the top is golden brown, about 10 minutes.

LiNGUINI WiTH CLAM SAUCE SERVES 4

- > 18 littleneck clams
- > ½ cup (120 ml) extra-virgin olive oil, divided
- > 1 pound (454 g) shrimp, peeled and deveined (optional)
- > Salt, to taste
- > Pepper, to taste
- > 1 Basil Flavor Bomb
- > 8-ounce (235 ml) bottle clam juice
- > 6½-ounce (184 g) can chopped clams (optional)
- > 1-pound (454 g) box linguini

RECiPE VARiATiON

If you'd like a red clam sauce, add a 15-ounce (425 g) can of crushed tomatoes to the sauce and simmer with the chopped clams for about 20 minutes.

1. Submerge the clams in a bowl of water, scrub them with a brush, and rinse.

2. Heat a medium saucepan over medium-high heat. If using the shrimp, add a swirl of the olive oil and sauté the shrimp for a minute on each side. Season with salt and pepper, remove the shrimp from the pan, and set aside.

3. Add the remaining olive oil, the Basil Flavor Bomb, and the clam juice to the pan. Simmer for 1 minute, stirring to combine. Bring a large pot of salted water to a boil for the linguini.

4. Add the scrubbed clams to the saucepan. Cover the pan (if you have a glass lid, you can watch!) and steam the clams until they open, about 5 minutes. Discard any clams that do not open.

5. As soon as the clams are open, remove them from the pan and set aside; clams overcook very quickly and get rubbery. (Incidentally, the clams are delicious right now with a little pan sauce!)

6. Add the chopped clams (if using) to the sauce, and gently simmer for 2 minutes. Return the shrimp to the saucepan.

7. Boil the linguini until al dente. Drain and place in a pasta serving bowl.

8. Spoon the sauce over the linguini and toss. Add the clams to the bowl, spooning some sauce over them. (Alternatively, you can remove the clams from their shells and add them to the sauce right before serving.) Serve immediately.

BASIL FLAVOR BOMB

STUFFED MUSHROOMS

SERVES 4 TO 6

> - 1 pound (454 g) white mushrooms (at least 24 large mushrooms)
> - ½ cup (120 ml) extra-virgin olive oil, divided, plus more for drizzling
> - 2 tablespoons (30 g) unsalted butter
> - Salt, to taste
> - Pepper, to taste
> - 2 tablespoons (30 ml) soy sauce
> - 1 Basil Flavor Bomb
> - 2 cups (120 g) fresh bread crumbs
> - ½ cup (50 g) grated Parmesan cheese
> - 2 tablespoons (31 g) part-skim ricotta cheese (full-fat is fine, too)

1. Preheat the oven to 350°F (180°C, or gas mark 4).

2. Remove the mushroom caps from the stems. To avoid broken mushrooms, gently use your thumb to push the stem to the side while cupping the mushroom in your other palm.

3. Trim the ends of the mushroom stems, rinse the stems, and finely chop them by hand or in a food processor.

4. Rinse, brush, and paper towel dry the mushroom caps. Place on a rimmed baking sheet with a drizzle of olive oil, and bake for about 8 minutes. They will shrink a bit and release their juices. Set aside, reserving the juices. Increase the oven temperature to 375°F (190°C, or gas mark 5).

5. Heat the butter and ¼ cup (60 ml) olive oil in a medium sauté pan over medium to medium-high heat. Add the chopped mushroom stems, salt, and pepper, and sauté until lightly browned. Then add the soy sauce, about a tablespoon (15 ml) of the reserved mushroom juice, and the Basil Flavor Bomb. Reduce the heat to medium and continue sautéing until the juice is reduced and the mixture is fragrant, 2 to 3 minutes.

6. Remove the sauté pan from the heat. Add the bread crumbs and grated Parmesan and blend. Add the ricotta and blend, adding more mushroom juice and the remaining ¼ cup (60 ml) olive oil as you mix, so the stuffing is not dry. Taste for seasoning, and add salt and pepper if needed.

7. Stuff the mushroom caps and drizzle them with olive oil. Bake the stuffed mushrooms for 5 minutes, or until lightly brown on top.

BASIL FLAVOR BOMB
QUINOA BALLS MAKES 8 BALLS

- > 1 cup (170 g) quinoa
- > 2 cups (475 ml) water or chicken broth (for denser quinoa, use 1¾ cups/425 ml)
- > 1 Basil Flavor Bomb
- > 8 ounces (225 g) fontina cheese
- > 1 egg, beaten
- > ¼ cup (30 g) all-purpose unbleached flour, for dredging
- > ¼ cup (60 ml) extra-virgin olive oil

1. Rinse the quinoa in a mesh strainer. Put the quinoa in a medium saucepan with the water or broth and bring to a boil. Reduce the heat to a simmer, cover, and cook until all the liquid is absorbed, 10 to 15 minutes.

2. Stir in the Basil Flavor Bomb. Let the quinoa sit until cool enough to handle.

3. Shape the quinoa into 8 balls, each about 1½ inches (4 cm) in diameter.

4. Cut the fontina into 8 cubes. Make an indent in each quinoa ball with your finger, insert a fontina cube in the middle, and roll it to cover the cheese.

5. Dip the quinoa balls in the beaten egg and dredge in the flour.

6. Heat the olive oil in a small frying pan over medium to medium-high heat and cook the balls until golden brown, about 3 minutes, turning often to color all sides. Serve immediately.

ROSEMARY FLAVOR BOMB

MAKES 14 OUNCES (392 G)

- 2 lemons
- ½ cup (68 g) pignoli (pine nuts)
- ¾ cup (180 ml) extra-virgin olive oil, divided
- ½ cup (75 g) roughly chopped garlic
- 1½ cups (40 g) fresh rosemary, stemmed and packed
- 1 cup (60 g) parsley, stemmed and packed
- Salt, to taste
- Pepper, to taste

1. Zest the lemons onto wax paper, and then squeeze the lemons for juice. You should have 2 tablespoons (12 g) grated lemon zest and ½ cup (120 ml) lemon juice. Set aside.

2. Lightly toast the pignoli in a dry medium sauté pan over medium heat for 2 to 3 minutes. Remove from the pan and set aside.

3. Add 6 tablespoons (90 ml) olive oil to the same pan and lightly sauté the garlic over medium heat until fragrant, about 2 to 3 minutes. Remove from the pan and set aside.

4. Pulse the rosemary and parsley in a food processor to roughly chop, then add the lemon zest and juice, pignoli, garlic, remaining 6 tablespoons (90 ml) olive oil, and salt and pepper to the food processor. Pulse again to the desired consistency. Do not purée.

5. Spoon the pesto into ice cube trays or small containers, or onto a wax paper–lined baking sheet or tray, and freeze. Once frozen, transfer the Flavor Bombs to an airtight container or a resealable freezer bag.

ROSEMARY FOCACCIA SERVES 4 TO 6

> - 1 cup (150 g) grape tomatoes or cherry tomatoes (about 12 tomatoes)
> - 2 tablespoons (30 ml) extra-virgin olive oil, plus more for greasing, thinning, and drizzling
> - Salt, to taste
> - Pepper, to taste
> - 1-pound (454 g) package prepared pizza dough, at room temperature (if frozen, defrost according to package instructions)
> - 1 Rosemary Flavor Bomb
> - 12 Kalamata olives or other oil-cured pitted olives, halved

1. Preheat the oven to 375°F (190°C, or gas mark 5).

2. Rinse and dry the tomatoes, and cut in half. Drizzle with 2 tablespoons (30 ml) olive oil, sprinkle with salt and pepper, toss, and spread in a single layer on a rimmed baking sheet. Roast for 15 minutes, or until browned and sizzling.

3. Grease an approximately 10 × 12-inch (25 × 30 cm) baking sheet with olive oil and spread the pizza dough out on it with your fingertips. Don't give up if it retracts when stretched; it will stay spread eventually. Let the dough rest for 10 minutes.

4. Thin the Rosemary Flavor Bomb with enough extra-virgin olive oil to be pourable.

5. Punch dents in the pizza dough with your fingertips. Brush it with the Rosemary Flavor Bomb–oil mixture; dot it all over with olives and tomatoes; drizzle on more olive oil; and let it rise for 30 more minutes.

6. Preheat the oven to 450°F (230°C, or gas mark 8).

7. Sprinkle the pizza with salt and pepper, and bake for 10 minutes. Then, lower the oven to 350°F (180°C, or gas mark 4) and bake for 10 more minutes, or until golden brown. Cool the pizza on a wire rack, so the bottom dries and crisps.

ROASTED RACK OF LAMB SERVES 3 TO 4

> - 2 racks (1½ pounds/680 g) of lamb
> - ¼ cup (60 ml) extra-virgin olive oil, divided
> - Salt, to taste
> - Pepper, to taste
> - 1 cup (60 g) fresh bread crumbs
> - 1 Rosemary Flavor Bomb

1. Preheat the oven to 425°F (220°C, or gas mark 7).

2. Brush the racks of lamb with 2 tablespoons (30 ml) olive oil, and sprinkle with salt and pepper. Sear the racks in a large frying pan over medium-high heat for about 1 minute on each side, until brown.

3. In a small bowl, blend together the bread crumbs, the Rosemary Flavor Bomb, and the remaining 2 tablespoons (30 ml) olive oil. Add salt and pepper to taste.

4. Coat the racks of lamb with the rosemary bread crumb mixture, patting it on to stick. Place in a roasting pan.

5. Roast lamb for 15 to 20 minutes, crust side up, or until the internal temperature reaches 130°F (55°C) for medium rare (cook longer for more well-done meat). Let the racks rest for 5 to 10 minutes before slicing.

ROSEMARY FLAVOR BOMB

ROSEMARY ROASTED POTATOES SERVES 4

> 1 Rosemary Flavor Bomb
> ½ to ¾ cup (120 to 175 ml) extra-virgin olive oil
> 2 to 3 pounds (1 to 1.5 kg) fresh or frozen potato wedges
> Salt, to taste
> Pepper, to taste

CHEF'S TIP

For extra crunch, toss the potatoes in a frying pan for 1 to 2 minutes before serving.

1. Preheat the oven to 400°F (200°C, or gas mark 6).

2. In a measuring cup, blend the Rosemary Flavor Bomb with the olive oil.

3. If using fresh potatoes, slice them in half and then into thirds or quarters for even-sized wedges. Microwave them on high power for 8 to 10 minutes to tenderize, and then spread in a single layer on a baking sheet. If using frozen potatoes, spread in a single layer on a baking sheet and allow to defrost at room temperature for about 15 minutes.

4. Bake the potatoes for 15 minutes. Remove from the oven and toss with the Rosemary Flavor Bomb mixture, salt, and pepper, and then return to the oven for 30 to 40 minutes longer, turning the pan halfway, until the exteriors of the potatoes are browned and the interiors are tender.

SAGE FLAVOR BOMB

MAKES 14 OUNCES (392 G)

- ½ cup (50 g) pecans
- ¾ to 1 cup (180 to 235 ml) extra-virgin olive oil, divided
- ¾ cup (106 g) roughly chopped shallots
- 2 cups (80 g) sage, stemmed and packed
- 1 cup (60 g) parsley, stemmed and packed
- Salt, to taste
- Pepper, to taste

1. Lightly toast the pecans in a dry medium sauté pan over medium heat for about 3 minutes. Remove from the pan and roughly chop by hand or by pulsing in a food processor. Set aside.

2. Add half of the olive oil to the same pan and lightly sauté the shallots over medium heat until fragrant, about 2 minutes. Remove from the pan and set aside.

3. Pulse the sage and parsley in a food processor to roughly chop. Add the pecans, shallots, remaining olive oil, and salt and pepper to the food processor. Pulse again to the desired consistency. Do not purée.

4. Spoon the pesto into ice cube trays or small containers, or onto a wax paper–lined baking sheet or tray, and freeze. Once frozen, transfer the Flavor Bombs to an airtight container or a resealable freezer bag.

SAGE FLAVOR BOMB

ROASTED PORK LOIN SERVES 4 TO 6

- › 2½ to 3 pounds (1 to 1.5 kg) boneless pork loin roast
- › Salt, to taste
- › Pepper, to taste
- › 1 Sage Flavor Bomb
- › 1 cup (225 g) mayonnaise

CHEF'S TiP

This is a pork LOIN roast, not a TENDERLOIN, which is the center of this roast. The loin is a little fattier and therefore juicier and more flavorful. A tenderloin is better for grilling.

I. Preheat the oven to 325°F (170°C, or gas mark 3).

2. Season the roast with salt and pepper. Blend the Sage Flavor Bomb with the mayonnaise, and slather the mixture all over the roast.

3. Place the roast in a roasting pan or on a rimmed baking sheet. Bake for about 1 hour, or until a meat thermometer inserted in the middle of the roast reads 145 to 150°F (63 to 66°C). It will continue cooking while resting.

4. Let the roast rest for 5 to 10 minutes before slicing.

FRIED CATFISH FILLETS

SERVES 2 TO 4

- 2 fillets catfish (8 to 10 ounces/227 to 283 g each)
- 1 Sage Flavor Bomb
- Salt, to taste
- Pepper, to taste
- 4 cups (240 g) fresh bread crumbs (or a mixture of panko and dried bread crumbs)
- 2 eggs
- 2 tablespoons (30 ml) half-and-half
- ½ cup (120 ml) canola or vegetable oil
- ¼ cup (½ stick/60 g) unsalted butter

1. Rinse the catfish fillets and pat dry.

2. Mix half the Sage Flavor Bomb, salt and pepper, and the bread crumbs in a shallow plate (suitable for breading the fillets).

3. Mix the other half of the Sage Flavor Bomb with the eggs, half-and-half, and salt and pepper in a bowl large enough to fit the fillets. Put the fillets in the bowl to marinate. Using a fork, pierce the fillets all around while in the egg batter, as if to tenderize them, turning them over to coat all sides.

4. Transfer one fillet at a time to the bread crumbs and coat evenly, pressing the breading firmly onto the fish. You want a nice thick breading. Transfer the breaded fillets to a tray.

5. In a large, nonstick frying pan, heat the canola or vegetable oil and butter over medium-high heat until a bread crumb sizzles when dropped in. Don't let the oil smoke.

6. Fry the fillets for 3 to 4 minutes on each side, until golden brown. Use two spatulas to turn the fillets over gently; they are large, and you don't want them dropping and splattering hot oil.

7. Place the fried fillets on a platter and sprinkle with salt. Portion at the table.

CHEF'S TIP

Catfish is often served in small, cut strips that are overcooked and dry. Keeping the fillets whole retains the juiciness, and the crunch you get from the fresh bread crumbs is incomparable.

SAGE FLAVOR BOMB

BAKED CHICKEN BREASTS

SERVES 3 TO 4

> 1 Sage Flavor Bomb
> 1 Mirepoix Flavor Bomb (page 102)
> ½ cup (120 ml) extra-virgin olive oil or ½ cup (1 stick/ 120 g) butter, softened
> 6 boneless, skinless chicken breasts (6 ounces/170 g each)
> Salt, to taste
> Pepper, to taste

LEFTOVERS?

Use baked chicken to make a great chicken salad. To make a chicken pot pie or chicken à la king, cube the chicken, mix it with 2 Béchamel Flavor Bombs (page 116), and simmer it with the chicken's pan juices and ½ cup (120 ml) half-and-half. Serve with noodles for chicken à la king, or add cooked or canned carrots and potatoes and spoon into a prebaked pastry crust (page 69) for pot pie (bake for 10 minutes).

1. Preheat the oven to 325°F (170°C, or gas mark 3).

2. In a small bowl, mix the Sage Flavor Bomb and the Mirepoix Flavor Bomb with the olive oil or softened butter.

3. Trim the chicken breasts of any fat or cartilage, rinse, and pat dry. Arrange the chicken in a single layer in a baking pan.

4. Slather the Flavor Bomb mixture over the chicken to coat evenly. Sprinkle the chicken with salt and pepper. Cover the pan with aluminum foil and bake for 30 to 40 minutes, or until the internal temperature reaches 165°F (74°C), turning the pan at the halfway point. Remove the foil from the pan and bake for an additional 10 minutes to brown the chicken.

THAi FLAVOR BOMB

MAKES 14 OUNCES (392 G)

- ¾ cup (180 ml) extra-virgin olive oil, divided
- ½ cup (70 g) roughly chopped garlic
- 2 cups (40 g) Thai basil (or Italian basil), stemmed and packed
- 1 cup (60 g) cilantro, stemmed and packed
- ½ cup (120 ml) coconut milk
- ½ cup (50 g) sliced lemongrass
- ¼ cup (60 ml) lime juice (juice of 1 lime with some pulp)
- 3 tablespoons (18 g) peeled and roughly chopped fresh ginger
- 2 tablespoons (30 ml) fish sauce
- 2 tablespoons (30 ml) soy sauce
- 2 tablespoons (32 g) peanut butter
- 2 teaspoons red pepper flakes
- ½ teaspoon curry powder
- Salt, to taste
- Pepper, to taste

1. Heat 6 tablespoons (90 ml) olive oil in a medium saucepan over medium heat, and then lightly sauté the garlic until fragrant, about 2 to 3 minutes. Remove from the pan and set aside.

2. Pulse the basil and cilantro in a food processor to roughly chop, and then add all the other ingredients, including the garlic and remaining 6 tablespoons (90 ml) olive oil. Pulse again to the desired consistency. Do not purée.

3. Spoon the pesto into ice cube trays or small containers, or onto a wax paper–lined baking sheet or tray, and freeze. Once frozen, transfer the Flavor Bombs to an airtight container or a resealable freezer bag.

CHEF'S TiP

To prep lemongrass, trim the top and base of the stalk. Cut off enough of the bottom until the purple rings are visible. You want to use only the bottom 4 inches (10 cm) or so. Then peel off any dry or tough outer layers before slicing into thin rings for the food processor.

THAI FLAVOR BOMB

SHRIMP & SUGAR SNAP PEA STIR-FRY SERVES 4

> 1 pound (454 g) large shrimp, peeled and deveined (16 count are nice)
> 1 pound (454 g) large sea scallops
> Salt, to taste
> Pepper, to taste
> 2 tablespoons (30 ml) extra-virgin olive oil, divided
> 1 Thai Flavor Bomb

> 1 tablespoon (15 ml) coconut milk
> 1 tablespoon (15 ml) soy sauce
> ½ teaspoon cumin
> ¼ teaspoon curry powder
> 1-pound (454 g) bag frozen sugar snap peas, defrosted (or fresh)
> 1-pound (454 g) bag frozen red peppers, defrosted (or fresh)

CONTINUED > > >

1. Rinse and dry the shrimp and scallops, keeping them separate. Season both with salt and pepper.

2. Heat 1 tablespoon (15 ml) olive oil in a large sauté pan over medium heat and sear the scallops for 2 minutes on each side. They should get a nice golden brown crust. Remove from the pan and set aside on a platter.

3. Add the remaining 1 tablespoon (15 ml) olive oil to the pan. Sauté the shrimp until they develop some color, about 1 minute on each side. Remove from the pan and set aside on the platter with the scallops.

4. The shrimp and scallops will release some juices onto the platter. Add the juices to the pan with the Thai Flavor Bomb, coconut milk, soy sauce, cumin, and curry powder. Let this pan sauce simmer to reduce a bit, 3 to 5 minutes.

5. Add the sugar snap peas and red peppers to the pan, and toss with the sauce. Add fresh cracked pepper and taste for salt, adding more if needed.

6. Return the shrimp and scallops to the pan, and toss them to coat with pan sauce and mix with the vegetables. Serve the stir-fry on the platter.

LEFTOVERS?

Add a can of water chestnuts, chop up the stir-fry, and mix in a tablespoon (16 g) of peanut butter. Then stuff into lettuce leaves, wonton wrappers, or spring-roll wrappers.

THAI CHICKEN NOODLE SOUP

SERVES 2 TO 4

- › 1 pound (454 g) skinless chicken thighs
- › 2 Thai Flavor Bombs
- › 2 tablespoons (30 ml) vegetable oil (or extra-virgin olive, coconut, or canola oil)
- › 6 cups (1.4 L) water
- › 14½-ounce (430 ml) can low-sodium chicken broth
- › 1 cup (235 ml) coconut milk
- › 1 tablespoon (15 ml) soy sauce
- › 1-pound (454 g) bag frozen Asian-style vegetables (defrosted)
- › 6 ounces (170 g) tofu (silken), diced
- › 8-ounce (225 g) bag soba noodles (Japanese buckwheat noodles)
- › Salt, to taste
- › Pepper, to taste
- › Sliced scallions, grated fresh ginger, or lime juice, for garnish

1. In a large soup pot over medium heat, sauté the chicken thighs with the Thai Flavor Bombs and oil for about 5 minutes.

2. Add the water, chicken broth, coconut milk, and soy sauce to the pot. Reduce the heat to low and simmer soup for about 90 minutes, stirring occasionally.

3. Remove the chicken from the broth with a slotted spoon. Let the chicken sit until cool enough to handle, and then shred or chop into small pieces. Set aside.

4. Add the vegetables and diced tofu to the broth and continue simmering.

5. Bring a large pot of salted water to a boil. Boil the soba noodles for 5 minutes and then drain. Add the noodles and chopped chicken to the soup.

6. Taste the soup and add salt and pepper if needed. Garnish the soup with sliced scallions, grated ginger, or a squeeze of lime juice.

TEX-MEX FLAVOR BOMB

MAKES 14 OUNCES (392 G)

- 1 cup (130 g) chopped cashews
- ¾ cup (180 ml) extra-virgin olive oil, divided
- ¾ cup (120 g) roughly chopped yellow onion (about 1 medium onion)
- 2 cups (120 g) cilantro, stemmed and packed
- 1 cup (60 g) flat leaf parsley, stemmed and packed
- 1 small jalapeño pepper, roughly chopped (keep seeds for extra heat)
- ½ cup (120 ml) lime juice (juice of 2 limes with some pulp)
- 1 teaspoon chili powder
- 1 teaspoon cayenne pepper
- Salt, to taste
- Pepper, to taste

1. Lightly toast the cashews in a dry medium sauté pan over medium heat for about 3 minutes. Remove from the pan and set aside.

2. Heat 6 tablespoons (90 ml) olive oil in the same pan over medium heat, and then sauté the onion until caramelized, about 20 minutes. Remove from the heat and set aside.

3. Pulse the parsley and cilantro in a food processor to roughly chop, and then add all the other ingredients, including the cashews, onions, and remaining 6 tablespoons (90 ml) olive oil. Pulse again to the desired consistency. Do not purée.

4. Spoon the pesto into ice cube trays or small containers, or onto a wax paper–lined baking sheet or tray, and freeze. Once frozen, transfer the Flavor Bombs to an airtight container or a resealable freezer bag.

TEX-MEX FLAVOR BOMB

TEXAS TOAST PANINI

MAKES 4 PANINI

- › 1 filet mignon steak (6 ounces/170 g), sliced into about 12 slices
- › Salt, to taste
- › Pepper, to taste
- › 1 Tex-Mex Flavor Bomb, divided
- › ¼ cup (60 ml) extra-virgin olive oil
- › 1-pound (454 g) bag frozen multicolor peppers
- › 2 to 4 tablespoons (15 to 30 g) chipotle peppers in adobo (depending on the heat you want)
- › 4¼-ounce (127 g) can diced green chiles
- › 8 slices Texas Toast bread (available in the grocery freezer case, already buttered)
- › 8 slices pepper Jack cheese

1. Sprinkle the filet slices with salt and pepper.

2. Blend half of the Tex-Mex Flavor Bomb with the olive oil. Marinate the filet in the oil for at least 1 hour.

3. Defrost the peppers. Drain any liquid and mix them with the chipotle, chiles, and the remaining half of the Tex-Mex Heat Flavor Bomb.

4. Sear the filet slices in a large frying pan over medium to medium-high heat until browned but still rare to medium-rare.

5. Assemble the panini. On a slice of Texas Toast, start with a slice of cheese, then the filet, then the pepper mixture, then another slice of cheese, and then a top bread slice. Repeat for four panini.

6. Heat a grill pan, if you have one (it makes awesome-looking grill marks on the bread). If not, use a nonstick frying pan. The pan should be hot enough to brown the bread, but don't let the panini burn! Place each sandwich on the hot grill pan or nonstick frying pan, and brown each side for 1 minute or so, using a bacon press or small frying pan to flatten and press down the sandwich.

CHEF'S TIP

I like filet mignon for this recipe because it's the most tender cut of steak for a sandwich. Plus, one filet steak goes a long way in this recipe. Slightly freeze the raw steak for easier slicing.

TEX-MEX LASAGNA

SERVES 4

- 2 pounds (1 kg) ground beef
- 1 teaspoon baking soda
- 1 teaspoon salt, plus more to taste
- 6 tablespoons (90 ml) water, divided
- 1 Umami Flavor Bomb (page 70) or 1 teaspoon soy sauce
- 2 Tex-Mex Flavor Bombs
- ½ cup (120 ml) beef broth
- ½ teaspoon cayenne pepper
- ½ teaspoon cumin
- ½ teaspoon paprika
- Pepper, to taste
- 28-ounce (794 g) can crushed tomatoes
- 12-ounce (340 g) bag wide egg noodles
- 4 Béchamel Flavor Bombs (page 116) or ½ cup (120 ml) Béchamel Sauce (page 74)
- ¼ cup (25 g) grated Parmesan cheese
- 8-ounce (225 g) bag shredded Mexican cheese blend

1. In a bowl, toss the ground beef with the baking soda, salt, and 2 tablespoons (30 ml) water until thoroughly combined. Set aside for 20 minutes.

2. Brown the ground beef in a large, deep skillet over medium heat, breaking it up into small pieces.

3. Add the Umami and Tex-Mex Flavor Bombs, beef broth, cayenne, cumin, paprika, salt, and pepper to the skillet. Bring to a simmer for a few minutes, stirring often, to reduce a bit and infuse flavors.

4. Add the crushed tomatoes and simmer for 1 hour, with the lid ajar, stirring frequently. Add the remaining 4 tablespoons (60 ml) water to the sauce gradually as it simmers and reduces. The sauce will be thick, so adding some liquid as it cooks is necessary to keep it sauce-like.

5. Boil the noodles in a large pot of salted water for about 8 minutes, or until al dente. Reserve ¼ cup (60 ml) noodle water, then drain. Return the noodles to the pot, and toss with the Béchamel Flavor Bombs and Parmesan cheese to coat noodles. Add the reserved noodle water to smooth the white sauce.

6. Preheat the oven to 325°F (170°C, or gas mark 3).

7. Lightly grease a 10 × 12-inch (25 × 30 cm) baking dish. Starting with the noodles, then the beef sauce, and then the shredded cheese, make layers in the baking dish. Top with the shredded cheese and a drizzle of sauce.

8. Cover the baking dish with aluminum foil greased with canola oil or cooking spray (so the cheese doesn't stick), and bake for 30 to 40 minutes, or until bubbling.

TEX-MEX SLOW COOKER BEANS SERVES 4 TO 6

> 1 pound (454 g) dried beans (pinto and navy bean mix), soaked overnight, drained, and rinsed
> 1 Tex-Mex Flavor Bomb
> ¼ cup (60 ml) maple syrup
> ¼ cup (60 g) brown sugar
> 2 Mirepoix Flavor Bombs (optional, page 102)
> 1 tablespoon (15 ml) vegetable oil or bacon grease
> 2 tablespoons (30 g) ketchup
> 1 tablespoon (16 g) tomato paste
> 1 tablespoon (15 ml) Worcestershire sauce
> 1 tablespoon (16 g) Dijon mustard
> ½ teaspoon ground cinnamon
> 1 cup (235 ml) water, divided
> 3 or 4 slices cooked maple bacon, crumbled

1. Put all the ingredients (except the maple bacon) and ½ cup (120 ml) water in a slow cooker. Cook on high for 2 hours.

2. Turn the slow cooker to low, and cook an additional 10 hours, stirring occasionally and adding the remaining water gradually, as needed.

3. Serve garnished with the crumbled maple bacon.

CHEF'S TiP

To speed things up, after soaking the beans overnight, bring them to a boil, cover, remove from heat, and let stand for 2 hours. Doing this cuts the cooking time in half, to 6 hours. Or you can use canned beans and cut the cooking time down to 2 to 3 hours—just don't expect the same rich flavor.

CHiMiCHURRi FLAVOR BOMB

MAKES 14 OUNCES (392 G)

- ¾ cup (175 ml) extra-virgin olive oil, divided
- ½ cup (75 g) roughly chopped garlic
- ½ cup (75 g) roughly chopped shallots
- 2 cups (120 g) cilantro, stemmed and packed
- 1 cup (60 g) flat-leaf parsley, stemmed and packed
- ½ cup (32 g) minced fresh or ¼ cup (12 g) dried oregano leaves
- ⅓ cup (80 ml) red wine vinegar
- 1 teaspoon red pepper flakes
- Salt, to taste
- Pepper, to taste

1. Heat 6 tablespoons (90 ml) olive oil in a medium saucepan over medium heat, and then lightly sauté the garlic and shallots until fragrant, about 2 to 3 minutes. Remove from the pan and set aside.

2. Pulse the cilantro, parsley, and oregano in a food processor to roughly chop, and then add all the other ingredients, including the garlic and shallots and remaining 6 tablespoons (90 ml) olive oil to the food processor. Pulse again to the desired consistency. Do not purée.

3. Spoon the pesto into ice cube trays or small containers, or onto a wax paper–lined baking sheet or tray, and freeze. Once frozen, transfer the Flavor Bombs to an airtight container or a resealable freezer bag.

CHIMICHURRI FLAVOR BOMB
CHICKEN
SCARPARIELLO SERVES 4 TO 6

> 1 pound (454 g) new red potatoes, cut in half
> ¾ cup (175 ml) extra-virgin olive oil or vegetable oil, divided
> Salt, to taste
> Pepper, to taste
> 1 ring (1 pound/454 g) sweet sausage (parsley and cheese flavor)
> 1 ring (1 pound/454 g) hot sausage
> 4 pounds (1.8 kg) chicken legs and thighs, cut in half (have your butcher do this), or 2 whole fryers, cut into 12 pieces each (leaving most skin on)

> 8 garlic cloves, peeled and lightly smashed
> 2 Chimichurri Flavor Bombs (use 3 for a stronger flavor)
> ¼ cup (60 ml) chicken broth
> ¼ cup (60 ml) lemon juice
> 2 to 4 tablespoons (30 to 60 ml) white wine or vermouth (optional)

CONTINUED > > >

1. Preheat the oven to 400°F (200°C, or gas mark 6).

2. Toss the potatoes with 2 tablespoons (30 ml) oil, salt, and pepper. Spread them in a single layer on a baking sheet. Roast for 30 minutes, tossing halfway through. Remove from the oven and set aside. Reduce the oven temperature to 375°F (190°C, or gas mark 5).

3. Heat 2 tablespoons (30 ml) oil in a large skillet over medium heat. Add both sausage rings and brown them on each side, trying not to break them. Do not fully cook the sausage. Once they're browned, remove them from the skillet and set aside in a large baking pan.

4. Add 2 more tablespoons (30 ml) of oil to the skillet and brown the chicken over medium heat, turning often, until browned all over. Work in batches if necessary, and don't fully cook the chicken. Transfer the chicken from the skillet to the baking pan with the sausage.

5. Add the remaining 6 tablespoons (90 ml) oil and garlic cloves to the small pieces of chicken skin that are stuck to the skillet to create "cracklins." Sauté the chicken skin over medium heat until dark golden brown and crunchy, stirring often with a large metal spatula and scraping up the fond (a browned layer) and bits.

6. Add the Chimichurri Flavor Bombs, chicken broth, lemon juice, and white wine or vermouth (if using) to the skillet. Simmer for a few minutes to reduce to a glaze, adding more broth if necessary to have enough sauce. Taste for salt and pepper and adjust if needed.

7. Break the sausage rings into 2- or 3-inch (5 to 7.5 cm) pieces. Some of the cheese filling should be spilling out.

8. Add the potatoes to the baking pan with the chicken and sausage. Bake for 10 minutes.

9. Pour the pan sauce all over the baking pan and toss everything together. Return the baking pan to the oven for about 15 minutes, or until you hear it sizzle.

CHIMICHURRI FLAVOR BOMB
GRILLED RIB-EYE STEAK SERVES 2

> 1 tablespoon (15 ml) cornstarch
> 1 tablespoon (15 ml) kosher salt
> 2 boneless rib-eye steaks (10 ounces/284 g each), about ½ inch (13 mm) thick
> ½ cup (120 ml) water or beef broth
> 1 or 2 Chimichurri Flavor Bombs

1. Mix the cornstarch and salt together and rub on both sides of the steaks. Chill the steaks in the refrigerator for about 30 minutes.

2. Sear the steaks in a large, hot pan, for 2 to 3 minutes on each side, depending on how rare you prefer them.

3. Remove the steaks from the pan and let them rest uncovered while you make the sauce.

4. Using the same pan over medium to medium-high heat, combine the water or beef broth and the Chimichurri Flavor Bomb(s). Stir and simmer to reduce, 3 to 5 minutes.

5. Spoon the sauce over the steaks and serve immediately.

CHEF'S TIP

If your steaks are thick, bake them in a 275°F (140°C, or gas mark 1) oven for 20 minutes (rare) or 30 minutes (medium) instead. Then sear each side for a minute or two.

SPANISH SOFRITO
FLAVOR BOMB

HOLY TRINITY
FLAVOR BOMB

VEGETABLE-BLEND FLAVOR BOMBS

UMAMI
FLAVOR BOMB

MIREPOIX
FLAVOR BOMB

ITALIAN SOFFRITTO
FLAVOR BOMB

INDIAN CURRY
FLAVOR BOMB

SUPPENGRÜN
FLAVOR BOMB

SUPPENGRÜN FLAVOR BOMB

MAKES 36 OUNCES (1 KG)

- ¾ pound (340 g) carrots (about 6 medium-sized carrots), peeled
- ½ pound (225 g) celery root, peeled
- 14½-ounce (430 ml) can low-sodium beef, chicken, or vegetable broth (I use beef), divided
- 1 pound (454 g) leeks (about 5 leeks)
- 6 tablespoons (¾ stick/90 g) unsalted butter, divided
- ¼ cup (60 ml) extra-virgin olive oil
- ¾ pound (340 g) green cabbage
- ¼ cup (16 g) minced fresh dill
- 2 tablespoons (14 g) caraway seeds
- ½ cup (120 ml) water, if needed
- Salt, to taste
- Pepper, to taste

1. Chop the carrots and celery root into a uniform ½-inch (13 mm) dice. Microwave in a microwave-safe bowl with a little less than ¼ cup (60 ml) broth for 5 minutes, and let sit, covered, to tenderize while you prepare the leeks.

2. Remove and discard the outer leaves of the leeks, slice the leeks into ½-inch (13 mm) rings, and soak them in a large bowl of water to remove the dirt. Drain and rinse as needed. In a large, deep skillet, sauté the leeks in 3 tablespoons (45 g) butter and the olive oil for 5 minutes over medium heat. Add 1 cup (235 ml) broth to the skillet, reduce the heat to medium-low, and braise the leeks for 15 minutes, or until caramelized, stirring often.

3. Slice the cabbage and chop the inner portion, saving the outer wedges for the Kielbasa with Braised Cabbage (page 66).

4. Add the cabbage, carrots, and celery root with the broth, and the remaining broth and 3 tablespoons (45 g) butter to the pan with the leeks. Over low heat, simmer and braise the vegetables, covered, stirring often, for 30 minutes, or until very tender.

5. Uncover the pan, and add the dill and caraway. Raise the heat to medium and reduce the liquid until it becomes a glaze. Add some water if necessary (if the liquid reduces too quickly or the mixture seems dry). Taste for salt and pepper, and adjust if needed. Remove from the heat and set aside.

6. Let the mixture cool, and then spoon it into ice cube trays or small containers, or onto a wax paper–lined baking sheet or tray, and freeze. Once frozen, transfer the Flavor Bombs to an airtight container or a resealable freezer bag.

SUPPENGRÜN FLAVOR BOMB
COLCANNON SERVES 4 TO 6

> - 2 pounds (1 kg) Yukon Gold potatoes, skins on
> - ¾ cup (175 ml) heavy cream or milk
> - ½ cup (1 stick/120 g) unsalted butter, divided
> - 6 Suppengrün Flavor Bombs

DID YOU KNOW?

This is a traditional Irish dish usually served on Halloween, but you'll want to eat it every night!

1. Put the potatoes in a large pot, cover with water by about 1 inch (2.5 cm), and bring to a boil over high heat. Reduce the heat and simmer, covered, for 15 to 20 minutes, or until tender (the tines of a fork should easily pierce them). Drain the potatoes into a colander.

2. Wearing gloves so you don't burn your fingers, peel the potatoes; the skins should come off very easily. Put the potatoes through a ricer into a serving bowl.

3. In a small saucepan or the microwave, heat the heavy cream or milk and ¼ cup (½ stick/60 g) butter. Fold into the potatoes using a whisk.

4. In a small saucepan or the microwave, warm the Suppengrün Flavor Bombs with the remaining ¼ cup (½ stick/60 g) butter. Pour over the potatoes and serve immediately.

KIELBASA WITH BRAISED CABBAGE SERVES 4 TO 6

> - 1 pound (454 g) kielbasa
> - 6 tablespoons (¾ stick/ 90 g) unsalted butter or rendered bacon fat, divided
> - 6 tablespoons (90 ml) extra-virgin olive oil, divided
> - 3 large Yukon Gold potatoes
> - 8 Suppengrün Flavor Bombs, divided
> - 1½ pounds (680 g) green cabbage
> - 14½-ounce (430 ml) can beef, chicken, or vegetable broth
> - Water, as needed
> - Salt, to taste
> - Pepper, to taste

1. Slice the kielbasa on the diagonal so there is plenty of interior meat surface to sear. In a large frying pan over medium heat, warm 2 tablespoons (30 g) of butter and 2 tablespoons (30 ml) olive oil. Sear the kielbasa slices for 2 minutes on each side, or until golden. Remove the kielbasa from the pan and set aside.

2. Peel and dice the potatoes. Add 2 tablespoons (30 g) butter and 2 tablespoons (30 ml) olive oil to the pan and fry the potatoes over medium heat until crisp and golden, about 15 minutes, turning often with a spatula. Add 4 Suppengrün Flavor Bombs to the pan the last 5 minutes of the potatoes' cooking time. Remove the potatoes from the pan and set aside with the kielbasa.

3. Core the cabbage and chop the leaves into approximately 3-inch (7.5 cm) pieces. Add the cabbage, the remaining 2 tablespoons (30 g) butter, remaining 2 tablespoons (30 ml) olive oil, and remaining 4 Flavor Bombs to the pan. Cook the cabbage over medium-low heat, turning often, to get some color on it.

4. Preheat the oven to 375°F (190°C, or gas mark 5).

5. Add the broth to the pan with the cabbage. Simmer, uncovered, over medium-high heat, deglazing the pan with a spatula as the cabbage cooks and the broth reduces, 15 to 20 minutes. Add water if necessary, and lower the heat if the liquid reduces too quickly. The broth should turn to a glaze-like consistency. Taste for salt and pepper, and adjust if needed.

6. When the cabbage is tender, transfer it to a roasting pan, leaving the broth in the pan. Put the kielbasa and potatoes on top. Pour the broth reduction over, and bake for 10 to 15 minutes.

SUPPENGRÜN FLAVOR BOMB

POT PiE WiTH GUiNNESS STOUT & CHEDDAR SERVES 4

> ½ pound (225 g) white button mushrooms
> ¼ cup (½ stick/60 g) unsalted butter
> 1½ pounds (680 g) ground beef, pork, and veal meatloaf mix
> 3 tablespoons (24 g) all-purpose unbleached flour
> 2 cups (475 ml) beef broth
> 2 cups (475 ml) Guinness stout
> 4 Suppengrün Flavor Bombs

> 1 Umami Flavor Bomb (optional, page 70)
> ¼ cup (60 ml) mushroom broth (optional, see steps 1 to 3 of Umami Flavor Bomb, page 138)
> 1½ cups (225 g) fresh or frozen peas
> 8 ounces (225 g) shredded Cheddar, divided
> 1 prepared pie crust sheet (see recipe on page 69 or use store-bought, not puff pastry)
> 1 egg yolk, beaten

CONTINUED >>>

1. Rinse, slice, and trim the mushrooms. Heat the butter in a large frying pan over medium-high to high heat. Sauté the mushrooms for about 10 minutes, stirring often, until browned and the liquid is evaporated. Remove the mushrooms from the pan and set aside.

2. Add the ground meat to the pan and sauté over medium heat until cooked through, approximately 7 minutes.

3. Sprinkle the meat with the flour, and stir until blended. Add the broth and stout, and simmer for 3 to 5 minutes, or until the sauce thickens and becomes silky. Add the Suppengrün Flavor Bombs and optional Bombs, if using, and stir.

4. Microwave the peas for about 5 minutes, and then add to the meat mixture. Add the mushrooms to the meat mixture and continue simmering. Fold half the Cheddar into the meat mixture.

5. Preheat the oven to 350°F (180°C, or gas mark 4).

6. Pour the meat mixture into an 8 x 8-inch (20 x 20 cm) glass baking dish. Scatter the remaining cheese on top. Lay the pie crust across the top, and crimp the edges to seal. Gently make slight slashes in the pie crust and brush with the beaten egg yolk.

7. Bake for 30 to 40 minutes, until the crust is deep golden brown.

PiE CRUST

SERVES 4 TO 6

- 2 cups (240 g) all-purpose unbleached flour
- ½ teaspoon salt
- ½ cup (1 stick/120 g) frozen unsalted butter, cut into cubes
- ¼ cup (52 g) very cold vegetable shortening (Crisco)
- 3 tablespoons (45 ml) very cold vodka
- 3 tablespoons (45 ml) ice water

RECiPE VARiATiON

You can also use this recipe for a dessert pie crust. Just add in 1 tablespoon (15 ml) of sugar with the flour and salt in step 1.

1. Pulse the flour and salt in a food processor to combine, two or three pulses.

2. Add the butter and shortening and process until clumps of dough just start to form. Scrape down the sides of the processor and pulse four more times. Transfer the dough to a large bowl.

3. Sprinkle the vodka and water over the dough, and fold it in with a spatula. Mix until the dough is tacky and holds together.

4. Transfer the dough to a countertop. Divide it into two equal-sized balls and flatten into 5-inch (12 cm) disks.

5. Wrap each disk in plastic wrap and refrigerate for at least 1 hour. The dough can stay in the refrigerator for a day or two.

6. To roll out the crust, place the chilled dough on a lightly floured countertop. Roll the dough outward from the center to the edge, using even, fairly firm pressure.

7. Using a dough scraper, lift the dough and turn it 90 degrees. Roll the dough outward again from the center. (Lightly flour underneath the dough as needed to prevent sticking.)

8. Repeat the process until the dough is about 3 inches (7.5 cm) wider than the pie plate.

9. To transfer the dough to the pie plate, lift and flip the edge of the dough onto the rolling pin and then turn it once or twice to loosely drape the dough around the pin.

10. Unroll the dough over the pie plate. Lift it around the edges and press into the corners of the plate, letting the excess dough hang over the edge. Trim the dough if necessary. Roll up the dough edge and crimp around the pie plate.

11. For a double-crust pie, repeat the rolling process with the second disk of dough. Roll the dough over the filled pie, press the edges together firmly to seal, and cut vents into the top. Bake according to the recipe instructions.

UMAMi FLAVOR BOMB

MAKES 36 OUNCES (1 KG)

- 3 ounces (85 g) dried mushrooms
- 3 cups (710 ml) boiling water
- 6 garlic cloves
- 1 large shallot
- ½ cup (1 stick/120 g) unsalted butter
- ¼ cup (60 ml) extra-virgin olive oil
- 1 pound (454 g) white button mushrooms
- ¼ teaspoon salt
- ¼ teaspoon pepper
- 2 tablespoons (32 g) low-sodium miso paste (I use red miso)
- 2 tablespoons (30 ml) soy sauce

1. Put the dried mushrooms in a bowl and cover with the boiling water, pushing them down with a spatula. Let soak for 30 minutes.

2. Chop the garlic and shallot in a food processor. Sauté them in a large frying pan with the butter and olive oil for 5 minutes over medium-low heat.

3. Strain the soaked mushrooms, reserving the mushroom broth. Strain the mushroom broth through a fine-mesh strainer and set aside. Chop the mushrooms in a food processor and add to the pan with the garlic-shallot mixture.

4. Raise the heat to medium-high, add the salt and pepper, and sauté the mixture for 30 minutes. Add the reserved mushroom liquid as needed, stirring often. Whisk together the miso and soy sauce with ¼ cup (60 ml) mushroom broth, and add it to the pan gradually as the mixture reduces, lowering the heat if necessary. Remove from the heat and set aside.

5. Let the mixture cool, and then spoon it into ice cube trays or small containers, or onto a wax paper–lined baking sheet or tray, and freeze. Once frozen, transfer the Flavor Bombs to an airtight container or a resealable freezer bag. Freeze any extra mushroom broth, too.

RECIPE VARIATION

To make a mushroom ragu, instead of chopping all of the mushrooms and combining them with the garlic and shallot in step 3, slice 1½ to 2½ cups (105 to 175 g) of the mushrooms and place into a separate medium pan. Add a scoop of the garlic-shallot mixture and sauté over medium heat for approximately 20 to 30 minutes.

UMAMI FLAVOR BOMB

UMAMI TAGLIATELLE PASTA SERVES 2

- > ½ pound (225 g) fresh or dried tagliatelle pasta
- > 2 tablespoons (30 ml) extra-virgin olive oil, plus more for drizzling
- > 4 Umami Flavor Bombs
- > 2 Béchamel Flavor Bombs (page 116) or ¼ cup (60 ml) Béchamel Sauce (page 74)
- > ¼ cup (25 g) grated Parmesan or Pecorino Romano, plus more for serving

1. Bring a large pot of salted water to a boil. Cook the pasta, according to package instructions, until al dente, reserving at least ½ cup (120 ml) pasta water before draining the pasta into a colander.

2. Add the olive oil, the Umami Flavor Bombs, and the Béchamel Flavor Bombs or Béchamel Sauce to the hot pasta pot. Stir to combine, adding a little pasta water to thin. Stir over low heat to create a thick sauce.

3. Return the pasta to the pot. Toss with the grated cheese and the sauce to coat, adding more pasta water if needed.

4. Transfer the pasta to a serving bowl. Drizzle with olive oil, sprinkle with a little grated cheese, and serve immediately.

CONTINUED > > >

BÉCHAMEL SAUCE MAKES 3 CUPS (705 ML)

> ½ cup (1 stick/120 g) unsalted butter
> 1 cup (120 g) seasoned flour (see Chef's Tip below)
> 2 cups (475 ml) 1% milk (or milk of your choice)
> 1 cup (235 ml) fat-free half-and-half
> ½ teaspoon ground nutmeg
> Salt, to taste
> Pepper to taste

1. In a medium saucepan over medium-low heat, melt the butter. Add the flour, whisking constantly, and cook for about 3 minutes.

2. Add the milk and half-and-half a cup (235 ml) at a time, whisking constantly, until all liquid is used.

3. Reduce the heat and let simmer, whisking constantly, for 3 to 5 more minutes. If the sauce seems too thick, add more milk as necessary.

4. Add the nutmeg, salt, and pepper, and stir.

5. The Béchamel Sauce is now ready to use. You may have more sauce than you need depending on the recipe; let the extra sauce cool and spoon it into ice cube trays or small containers and freeze.

CHEF'S TIP

I keep a batch of seasoned flour in my pantry at all times. This is the basic recipe, but I sometimes add lemon pepper, curry powder, cayenne, nutmeg, or any other dry spice, to my own taste, to change things up. Think of it as a "Flour Bomb."

> 1½ cups (180 g) all-purpose flour
> 1 teaspoon salt
> 1 teaspoon black pepper
> 1 teaspoon garlic powder

Mix ingredients together in a bowl and store in a container in your pantry, refrigerator, or freezer.

For gluten-free cooking, use garbanzo (chickpea), rice, or coconut flour.

POLENTA WiTH MUSHROOM RAGU

SERVES 2 TO 4

- 2 cups (475 ml) water
- 14½-ounce (430 ml) can low-sodium chicken broth
- 1 cup (163 g) polenta (you can substitute quick-cooking durum wheat semolina or traditional-style coarse yellow cornmeal)
- ¼ teaspoon salt
- ¼ cup (25 g) grated Parmesan or Pecorino Romano cheese (optional)
- 6 to 8 ounces (170 to 225 g) mushroom ragu (see Umami Flavor Bomb, page 70)
- Drizzle of extra-virgin olive oil (optional)

1. Combine the water and chicken broth in a medium saucepan and bring to a boil. Gradually add the polenta, whisking constantly.

2. Reduce the heat and simmer the polenta for 5 minutes (if using quick-cooking polenta) or up to 30 minutes (for traditional polenta), stirring frequently with a wooden spoon. Add the salt and grated cheese, if using, to the polenta.

3. Heat the mushroom ragu on the stovetop or in the microwave. Spoon the polenta onto a serving platter, and top with the mushroom ragu. Drizzle with olive oil, if desired. Serve immediately.

CHICKEN SORRENTINO WITH MARSALA SAUCE SERVES 4 TO 6

- > 8 boneless, skinless chicken breasts (6 ounces/170 g each)
- > Salt, to taste, plus additional for salting the eggplant
- > Pepper, to taste
- > 1 cup (120 g) seasoned flour (see Chef's Tip, page 74), divided
- > 6 tablespoons (¾ stick/90 g) unsalted butter, divided
- > ½ cup (120 ml) extra-virgin olive oil, divided

- > 1 pound (454 g) white button mushrooms, sliced
- > ½ cup (120 ml) Marsala wine
- > 14½-ounce (430 ml) can low-sodium chicken broth
- > 2 tablespoons (32 g) tomato paste
- > 4 Umami flavor Bombs
- > 1 large eggplant, peeled
- > ⅓ pound (150 g) thinly sliced prosciutto
- > 8 ounces (225 g) shredded mozzarella cheese

RECIPE VARIATION

Leave out the eggplant, prosciutto, and mozzarella for chicken Marsala. To make chicken Marsala, stop after step 6. Pour the sauce over the chicken cutlets and bake at 375° (190°C, or gas mark 5) for 5 to 10 minutes, or until the sauce is bubbling.

1. Trim, rinse, and pat dry the chicken breasts. Lay each chicken breast between sheets of plastic wrap and pound with the flat side of a meat tenderizer. Pound the thickest parts of each breast until they are of even thickness. If the cutlets seem too large, slice them in half.

2. Sprinkle the cutlets with salt and pepper. Dredge the cutlets in ½ cup (60 g) of the seasoned flour.

3. Heat ¼ cup (½ stick/60 g) butter and ¼ cup (60 ml) olive oil in a large frying pan over high heat until shimmering.

4. Working in batches, place the cutlets in the frying pan and cook for about 2 minutes per side, until all are nicely golden brown. (If the beginning batches of cutlets aren't as brown as the later ones, return them to the frying pan to coat with some of the browned flour just to get more color on them, about 20 seconds or so. All the cutlets should have a flavorful golden color.) Remove the cutlets from the pan and set them aside, covered, in a baking dish.

5. Add the remaining 2 tablespoons (30 g) butter to the frying pan. Sauté the mushrooms over high heat until tender and golden, 5 to 10 minutes.

6. Add the Marsala wine to the pan and stir to deglaze the pan. Add the chicken broth, tomato paste, and Umami Flavor Bombs. Simmer until the sauce thickens, at least 5 minutes.

7. Slice the eggplant into ¼-inch (6 mm) thick ovals, and lay on a rack in the sink. Sprinkle each eggplant slice with ¼ teaspoon salt and let sit for about 30 minutes.

8. Rinse the eggplant with the sink sprayer; you will see the brown, bitter eggplant liquid being sprayed away with the salt. Immediately dredge the eggplant slices in the remaining ½ cup (60 ml) seasoned flour.

9. Heat the remaining ¼ cup (60ml) olive oil in a large frying pan over medium heat. Fry the eggplant slices for 2 to 3 minutes on each side, until lightly golden brown. Place the eggplant on a paper towel–lined tray.

10. Preheat the oven to 375°F (190°C, or gas mark 5).

11. To assemble the Sorrentino, arrange the chicken cutlets in a single layer in the baking dish. Put a slice of eggplant on top of each cutlet, and then a spoon of sauce on top of the eggplant. Place a slice of prosciutto on top. Sprinkle handfuls of shredded mozzarella on top of the prosciutto, and then spoon the sauce and mushrooms over.

12. Bake the cutlets, tightly covered with aluminum foil, for 20 to 30 minutes, or until the cheese is melted and the sauce is bubbling.

UMAMI FLAVOR BOMB

BEEF WELLINGTON SERVES 4

> 2½ pounds (1 kg) beef tenderloin roast, at room temperature
> ¼ teaspoon salt
> ¼ teaspoon pepper
> 1 tablespoon (15 g) unsalted butter
> 8 Umami Flavor Bombs
> 1 sheet frozen puff pastry, thawed
> 1 egg yolk, beaten

CHEF'S TIP

This is a truly a luxurious dish and not as difficult to make as you may think.

1. Preheat the oven to 400°F (200°C, or gas mark 6).

2. Pat the tenderloin dry with paper towels, and sprinkle with salt and pepper. Heat the butter in a medium frying pan over medium-high heat, and sear the meat for about 2 minutes on each side. Remove the tenderloin from the pan and let cool to room temperature.

3. Use the Umami Flavor Bombs to coat the tenderloin top and sides.

4. Use a rolling pin to roll out the puff pastry sheet large enough to wrap around the tenderloin. Lay the pastry sheet over the tenderloin, on top of the Umami Flavor Bomb coating, and tuck it underneath. Carefully lift the tenderloin with a spatula and pinch the pastry dough underneath to overlap and seal the pastry. Make sure the dough is smooth all around the tenderloin.

5. Transfer the tenderloin to a rimmed baking sheet. Brush the pastry with the beaten egg. Make six 1-inch (2.5 cm) slits across the top with a sharp knife so steam can escape.

6. For a medium-rare tenderloin, bake until an instant-read thermometer inserted in the center reads 135°F (57°C), approximately 40 minutes. Remove the tenderloin from the oven and let rest for 10 minutes, loosely tented with aluminum foil, before slicing. Serve cut into ¾-inch (2 cm) thick slices.

SPANISH SOFRITO FLAVOR BOMB

MAKES 32 OUNCES (896 G)

- 1 garlic bulb, trimmed and peeled
- 1 cup (235 ml) extra-virgin olive oil
- 4 large yellow onions, trimmed and peeled
- 2 cubanelle peppers, trimmed and seeded
- 2 red bell peppers, trimmed and seeded
- 2 medium tomatoes or 4 plum tomatoes with juice from a can
- 1 cup (60 g) cilantro, stemmed and packed
- 1 cup (60 g) parsley, stemmed and packed
- 1 bay leaf
- ¼ teaspoon cayenne pepper
- ¼ teaspoon paprika
- ¼ teaspoon cumin
- ¼ teaspoon nutmeg
- Salt, to taste
- Pepper, to taste

1. Mince the garlic in a food processor. Heat the olive oil in a large frying pan over medium heat, and sauté the garlic until caramelized, about 5 minutes.

2. Chop the onions in a food processor. Add the onions to the pan with the garlic, lower the heat to medium-low, and sauté, covered, stirring occasionally, for about 20 minutes.

3. Chop the cubanelle and bell peppers in a food processor and then add to the pan.

4. If using fresh tomatoes, boil them in a large pot of water until soft. Purée the tomatoes in a food processor with the cilantro and parsley, and add to the pan. If using canned tomatoes, purée them in a food processor and add to the pan with juices.

5. Reduce the heat to low and simmer the mixture, uncovered, stirring often, for 20 minutes. Add the bay leaf, cayenne, paprika, cumin, nutmeg, and salt and pepper, and simmer for an additional 10 minutes. Remove from the heat. Remove and discard the bay leaf.

6. Let the mixture cool, and then spoon it into ice cube trays or small containers, or onto a wax paper–lined baking sheet or tray, and freeze. Once frozen, transfer the Flavor Bombs to an airtight container or a resealable freezer bag.

SLOW-COOKED PORK SHOULDER

SERVES 4 TO 6

> - 4 pounds (1.8 kg) bone-in pork shoulder
> - 1 tablespoon (15 ml) Cajun spice blend (see step 5 of Holy Trinity Flavor Bomb, page 86)
> - ¼ teaspoon salt
> - 6 Spanish Sofrito Flavor Bombs
> - ¼ cup (60 ml) vegetable oil
> - 3 cups (700 ml) water, divided
> - 2 tablespoons (30 ml) Worcestershire sauce
> - 1 tablespoon (15 ml) soy sauce

1. Preheat the oven to 275°F (140°C, or gas mark 1).

2. Rinse the pork shoulder, and pat dry. Score the top fat cap with a sharp paring knife, creating a diagonal checkerboard pattern.

3. In a Dutch oven over medium-high heat, sear the pork on all sides, about 2 minutes per side. Remove from the heat and season with the Cajun spice blend and salt.

4. Add the Spanish Sofrito Flavor Bombs, vegetable oil, 1 cup (235 ml) water, Worcestershire sauce, and soy sauce to the Dutch oven. Stir to mix.

5. Cover the Dutch oven. Cook the pork in the oven for 2½ hours, and then remove from the oven, uncover, and add an additional 1 cup (235 ml) water and stir. Do not baste the pork; basting will prevent the fat from crisping. Cover the Dutch oven and return to the oven for another 2½ hours, and then remove from the oven, uncover, and add the remaining 1 cup (235 ml) water and stir. Return to the oven, uncovered, for a final 1 hour of cooking. The pork will be very tender and shred easily.

6. The pork can be served sliced (with pan drippings as sauce), shredded for pulled pork sandwiches, or as carnitas (using pan drippings to moisten).

FRiED PORK CHOPS

SERVES 3 TO 4

- > 6 pork chops (8 ounces/227 g each), ½ inch (13 mm) thick
- > Salt, to taste
- > Pepper, to taste
- > ¼ teaspoon cumin
- > ¼ teaspoon cinnamon
- > Pinch of cayenne pepper
- > ⅓ cup (80 ml) plus ¼ cup (60 ml) milk, divided
- > 3 cups (150 g) panko
- > 1 cup (60 g) fresh bread crumbs
- > 6 Spanish Sofrito Flavor Bombs
- > ½ cup (120 ml) canola oil, for frying
- > 4 Béchamel Flavor Bombs (page 116)

1. Sprinkle the pork chops with salt, pepper, cumin, cinnamon, and cayenne. Marinate the chops in ⅓ cup (80 ml) milk for about 30 minutes.

2. Mix together the panko, bread crumbs, and Spanish Sofrito Flavor Bombs in a flat tray or plate suitable for breading the chops. Bread the pork chops by firmly pressing the panko mixture onto them; they should be thickly coated.

3. Heat the canola oil in a large frying pan over medium heat until shimmering. Fry the pork chops for 3 to 4 minutes on each side. Work in batches if necessary. Place the chops in the oven at its lowest temperature to keep warm.

4. In a small saucepan over medium heat, heat the Béchamel Flavor Bombs with the remaining ¼ cup (60 ml) milk to thin it out a bit.

5. Spoon the béchamel sauce over the chops, or serve in a gravy boat at the table.

CHEF'S TiP

Alternatively, to bake the pork chops, place the chops on a wire rack set in a shallow baking pan. Spray the chops with butter or oil spray and bake at 375°F (190°C, gas mark 5) for 30 to 40 minutes, or until the internal temperature reads 150°F (66°C) on an instant-read thermometer.

SPANISH CHICKEN WITH CASHEW PURÉE

SERVES 3 TO 4

- 3 pounds (1.4 kg) chicken legs and thighs
- 1 teaspoon salt
- ½ teaspoon pepper
- 2 tablespoons (30 ml) extra-virgin olive oil
- ⅔ cup (160 ml) sherry
- 1 cup (235 ml) chicken broth
- 4 Spanish Sofrito Flavor Bombs
- ¼ teaspoon ground cinnamon
- 2 tablespoons (30 g) unsalted butter
- 2 teaspoons lemon juice
- ½ cup (75 g) unsalted cashews
- 1 large pinch of saffron
- 2 tablespoons (8 g) chopped fresh parsley, for garnish (optional)

1. Rinse the chicken and pat dry. Season all sides with salt and pepper.

2. Heat the olive oil in a large ovenproof skillet over medium-high heat until shimmering. Add the chicken and brown on both sides, about 10 minutes. Transfer the chicken to a baking dish, and, when cool enough to handle, remove the skin from the chicken parts and discard. Remove any pieces of skin that may have stuck to the skillet.

3. Preheat the oven to 300°F (150°C, or gas mark 2).

4. Add the sherry to the skillet and deglaze, scraping up the brown bits. Stir until the sherry starts to thicken, about 2 minutes. Stir in the chicken broth and Spanish Sofrito Flavor Bombs, and simmer, stirring, for about 5 minutes to thicken. Add the cinnamon, butter, and lemon juice, and continue stirring for 2 minutes.

5. Return the chicken and any juices to the skillet. Bring to a simmer and braise the chicken for about 30 minutes, coating the pieces with sauce. Remove 1 cup (235 ml) pan liquid and set aside.

6. Cover the skillet with aluminum foil and put in the oven. (Alternatively, transfer the contents of the skillet to a baking dish.) Bake for about 1 hour, uncovering the dish for the last 15 minutes.

7. Pulse the cashews, saffron, and reserved pan liquid in a food processor or blender to make a purée. The purée should be fairly smooth, with bits of cashew.

8. Serve the chicken with the pan sauce and a dollop of cashew purée on top, and sprinkle with the parsley, if using.

HOLY TRINITY FLAVOR BOMB

MAKES 24 OUNCES (672 G)

- 4 large yellow onions
- 4 celery stalks
- 2 green bell peppers
- ¼ cup (60 ml) extra-virgin olive oil
- ¼ cup (½ stick/60 g) unsalted butter
- 3 teaspoons (15 ml) salt, divided
- 2 teaspoons black pepper, divided
- 3 tablespoons (21 g) paprika
- 2 tablespoons (30 ml) dried oregano
- 1 tablespoon (15 ml) dried basil
- 1 tablespoon (15 ml) cayenne pepper
- 1 tablespoon (15 ml) garlic powder
- 1 tablespoon (15 ml) onion powder
- 1 tablespoon (15 ml) white pepper

1. Chop the onions, celery, and peppers into ½-inch (13 mm) dice.

2. Heat the olive oil and butter in a large frying pan over medium-low heat, and add the onions. Cook the onions, covered, for 15 minutes.

3. Add the celery and peppers to the pan with the onions. Add 1 teaspoon each of salt and black pepper to the pan.

4. Cook the Holy Trinity mixture, covered, but stirring often, for about 45 minutes. Remove from the heat.

5. While the mixture cooks, create your Cajun/Creole spice blend by mixing together the paprika, oregano, basil, cayenne pepper, garlic powder, onion powder, and white pepper. Remove from the heat and set aside.

6. As the Holy Trinity mixture cools, add your Cajun/Creole seasoning by the tablespoon (15 ml), to taste. The blend will be used in future recipes, so don't overseason your Flavor Bomb. Add the remaining 2 teaspoons salt and 1 teaspoon black pepper to the Holy Trinity mixture.

7. Let the mixture cool, and then spoon it into ice cube trays or small containers, or onto a wax paper–lined baking sheet or tray, and freeze. Once frozen, transfer the Flavor Bombs to an airtight container or a resealable freezer bag.

DID YOU KNOW?

The Holy Trinity consists of onions, celery, and peppers, and is often used as a base in Cajun and Creole cooking.

SHRIMP PO' BOYS WITH TRINITY SLAW

SERVES 4

SHRIMP

> 1 pound (454 g) large shrimp, peeled and deveined
> ½ cup (60 g) seasoned flour (see Chef's Tip, page 74)
> 2 eggs
> 2 tablespoons (30 ml) fat-free half-and-half or milk
> 2 cups (56 g) cornflakes
> 1 teaspoon Cajun seasoning blend (see Holy Trinity Flavor Bomb, page 86)
> 1 cup (235 ml) canola oil, for frying

SLAW

> ½ pound (225 g) shredded cabbage or lettuce
> 4 Holy Trinity Flavor Bombs
> 3 tablespoons (42 g) mayonnaise
> 2 teaspoons coarse-grained mustard
> 1 teaspoon apple cider vinegar or lemon juice
> ½ teaspoon horseradish

SANDWICHES

> 4 soft rolls
> 2 tablespoons (30 g) unsalted butter, melted

CONTINUED > > >

1. To prepare the shrimp, rinse the shrimp and pat dry. Make a small slice along the bottom edge of each to butterfly.

2. Put the seasoned flour in a small, flat dish, suitable for dredging the shrimp. Beat together the eggs and half-and-half in a bowl.

3. Put the cornflakes in a resealable plastic bag and crumble with your fingers and light punches. Pour the crumbled cornflakes into a flat dish, suitable for breading the shrimp. Mix the Cajun seasoning into the cornflake crumbs.

4. Heat the canola oil in a large frying pan over medium heat until shimmering.

5. Dredge the shrimp in the flour, dip in the egg mixture, and bread with the cornflake crumbs. Firmly press the crumbs onto all sides of the shrimp.

6. Fry the shrimp over medium to medium-high heat, a few at a time, browning on all sides. (Be sure even to stand them up to brown each end for a minute or two.)

7. To make the slaw, combine all of the ingredients in a large bowl and keep covered until serving.

8. To assemble the sandwiches, hollow out the tops of the rolls to fit the shrimp and slaw. Brush each roll with the melted butter. Place 3 or 4 shrimp on each roll, and top with the slaw.

HOLY TRINITY FLAVOR BOMB
SHRIMP CREOLE SERVES 2 TO 4

- > 3 tablespoons (45 ml) vegetable oil
- > 2 tablespoons (15 g) seasoned flour (see Chef's Tip, page 74)
- > 4 Holy Trinity Flavor Bombs
- > 4 Spanish Sofrito Flavor Bombs (page 80) or 14½-ounce (411 g) can crushed tomatoes
- > ½ cup (120 ml) dry white wine (optional)
- > ½ cup (120 ml) water (1 cup (235 ml) if not using wine; omit entirely if using canned tomatoes)
- > 1 tablespoon (15 ml) Worcestershire sauce
- > 1 tablespoon (16 g) tomato paste
- > 1 teaspoon Cajun seasoning blend (see Holy Trinity Flavor Bomb, page 86)
- > 2 pounds (1 kg) large shrimp, peeled and deveined
- > 2 tablespoons (8 g) chopped parsley, for garnish
- > Salt, to taste
- > Pepper, to taste
- > Cooked rice, grits, polenta, or linguini, for serving

1. Heat the vegetable oil in a large skillet over medium heat until shimmering. Add the flour and cook, whisking constantly, until light brown, about 5 minutes.

2. Add the Holy Trinity Flavor Bombs and stir. Add the Spanish Sofrito Flavor Bombs or crushed tomatoes and stir. Add the wine (if using), water, Worcestershire sauce, tomato paste, and Cajun seasoning blend. Bring to a simmer. Reduce the heat to low, cover, and cook, stirring occasionally, for 20 to 30 minutes. The sauce should be thick.

3. Add the shrimp, raise the heat to medium, and simmer until the shrimp are cooked, about 5 minutes (depending on size). The shrimp will give off some liquid to thin the sauce a bit. Add the chopped parsley and salt and pepper to taste.

4. Serve over cooked rice, grits, polenta, or linguini.

HOLY TRiNiTY FLAVOR BOMB

ANDOUiLLE SAUSAGE & CHiCKEN GUMBO

SERVES 4 TO 6

- 2 pounds (1 kg) boneless, skinless chicken thighs
- Salt, to taste
- Pepper, to taste
- ¼ cup (60 ml) vegetable oil or bacon fat drippings
- 1 pound (454 g) andouille sausage, sliced into ¼-inch (6 mm) thick disks
- 2 tablespoons (30 g) unsalted butter
- ¾ cup (90 g) all-purpose unbleached flour
- 12 Holy Trinity Flavor Bombs

- 4 garlic cloves, minced
- 14½-ounce (411 g) can stewed tomatoes
- 14½-ounce (430 ml) can low-sodium chicken broth
- 1 tablespoon (15 ml) Worcestershire sauce
- 1 cup (235 ml) water, divided
- ½ teaspoon Cajun seasoning blend (see Holy Trinity Flavor Bomb, page 86)
- Cooked rice, for serving
- Sliced scallions, for garnish (optional)

1. Rinse the chicken thighs, pat dry, and slice into chunks. Season the chicken with salt and pepper.

2. Heat the vegetable oil or bacon fat in a large skillet over medium-high heat, and brown the chicken for about 5 minutes. Add the sliced sausage to the pan and lightly brown, turning with the chicken pieces, for 5 more minutes. Remove the chicken and sausage from the pan and set aside.

3. Add the butter to the pan and melt. Reduce the heat to low, and add the flour to the pan, stirring with a whisk to create a roux. Continue whisking the roux for up to 20 minutes, to develop a dark caramel color.

4. Add the Holy Trinity Flavor Bombs and the minced garlic to the roux, stirring for a minute or two.

5. Add the stewed tomatoes, chicken broth, Worcestershire sauce, and ½ cup (120 ml) water. Raise the heat and bring to a simmer. Continue cooking and stirring for about 10 minutes. Stir in the Cajun seasoning blend.

6. Return the chicken and sausage to the pan with any juices. Continue simmering and stirring the gumbo, uncovered, for 5 to 10 minutes. Add the remaining ½ cup (120 ml) water if it seems too thick.

7. Serve gumbo in a bowl with rice, and sprinkle with the sliced scallions, if using.

INDIAN CURRY FLAVOR BOMB

MAKES 34 OUNCES (952 G)

- ⅔ cup (160 ml) canola oil
- ⅓ cup coconut oil (80 ml) or coconut butter (73 g)
- 1 cinnamon stick, broken in half
- 4 whole cloves
- 2 whole star anise
- 1 garlic bulb, trimmed and peeled
- 2 pounds (1 kg) yellow onions (about 10 small onions), trimmed and peeled
- 2 teaspoons ground cumin
- 1 teaspoon ground turmeric
- ½ teaspoon ground cardamom
- ½ teaspoon ground cinnamon
- ½ teaspoon prepared curry powder (optional)
- ¼ teaspoon ground cloves
- ¼ teaspoon black pepper
- Pinch of cayenne pepper
- ½ teaspoon salt
- 2 tablespoons (32 g) tomato paste
- ¾ cup (175 ml) heavy cream
- 1 teaspoon sugar

1. Heat the canola and coconut oils in a large frying pan over medium heat. Add the cinnamon stick, cloves, and star anise, and let them sizzle for about 5 minutes, or until fragrant. The cinnamon stick will uncurl and the oil will develop a deep color. Remove the spices from the pan and discard or let cool and grind for future use. Let the oil cool for a few minutes.

2. Finely chop the garlic in a food processor. (Adding a little canola or olive oil to the food processor with the garlic will help it chop easily.) Set aside. Finely chop the onions in a food processor. Set aside.

3. Add the garlic to the cooled oil and sauté for 3 to 5 minutes over medium-low heat. Add the onions and cook for 30 minutes, covered, stirring occasionally.

4. While the onions cook, make the curry blend by mixing together the cumin, turmeric, cardamom, ground cinnamon, curry powder (if using), cloves, black pepper, and cayenne pepper in a small bowl.

5. Add the curry blend, 1 teaspoon at a time, to the onion mixture to taste. The blend will be used in future recipes, so don't overseason your Flavor Bomb. Continue cooking for 20 minutes longer, covered, stirring often. Uncover the mixture, add the salt, and cook for 10 more minutes, stirring often.

6. Transfer one half of the mixture to a bowl and let cool. Spoon it into ice cube trays or small containers for Plain Indian Curry Flavor Bombs. Freeze.

7. Add the tomato paste, heavy cream, and sugar to the remaining mixture in the pan and simmer for 3 to 5 minutes. Let cool and spoon into ice cube trays or small containers for Tomato Indian Curry Flavor Bombs. Freeze. Once frozen, transfer the Flavor Bombs to an airtight container or a resealable freezer bag.

INDIAN CURRY FLAVOR BOMB

CAULIFLOWER, PEAS & POTATO CURRY

SERVES 4

- > 3 medium Yukon Gold potatoes or 15-ounce (425 g) can diced potatoes
- > ¾ pound (340 g) fresh (about ½ head) or frozen cauliflower
- > 1½ cups (225 g) fresh or frozen peas
- > ¼ cup (60 ml) water
- > 2 tablespoons (30 ml) canola oil
- > 2 teaspoons curry blend (see step 4 of Indian Curry Flavor Bomb, page 94)
- > 2 plain Indian Curry Flavor Bombs
- > 1 cup (235 ml) coconut milk or heavy cream
- > 1-inch (2.5 cm) piece ginger, peeled and grated
- > Salt, to taste
- > Pepper, to taste

1. If using fresh potatoes, peel and dice them. If using fresh cauliflower, core, trim, and cut into small florets.

2. Put the potatoes, cauliflower, and peas in a microwave-safe bowl, sprinkle with the water, cover, and microwave on high power for approximately 6 minutes, or until tender. (If using canned potatoes, do not microwave them.)

3. Heat the canola oil in a large skillet over medium heat until shimmering. Add the curry spice blend and let it "bloom" (gently fry) for about 30 seconds, to develop the aroma. Add the Indian Curry Flavor Bombs, coconut milk, and grated ginger. Simmer for 2 minutes over medium heat to thicken.

4. Add the vegetables with their liquid to the skillet. Stir to coat the vegetables, and simmer for another 2 to 3 minutes. Taste for salt and pepper, and adjust if needed.

CHEF'S TIP

You can make this dish with fresh or frozen vegetables.

CHICKEN TIKKA MASALA SERVES 4

CHICKEN

> 2 pounds (1 kg) boneless, skinless chicken breasts or thighs
> 1 teaspoon curry blend (see step 4 of Indian Curry Flavor Bomb, page 94)
> 1 teaspoon salt
> 1 cup (245 g) plain Greek yogurt
> 2 tablespoons (30 ml) vegetable oil
> 1 tablespoon (10 g) minced fresh or ½ tablespoon (8 ml) dried garlic
> 1 tablespoon (8 g) grated ginger

SAUCE

> 2 tablespoons (30 g) unsalted butter
> 2 plain Indian Curry Flavor Bombs
> 1 tablespoon (15 g) tomato paste
> 1 tablespoon (15 ml) curry blend (see step 4 of Indian Curry Flavor Bomb, page 94)
> 15-ounce (425 g) can tomato sauce
> ½ cup (120 ml) heavy cream
> 1 large pinch of saffron

1. To prepare the chicken, trim the chicken, rinse, and pat dry. Cut it into 2-inch (5 cm) chunks. Season the chunks with the curry blend and salt, cover, and let rest for about 30 minutes.

2. In the meantime, make the sauce by heating the butter in a medium saucepan over medium heat. Add the Indian Curry Flavor Bombs, the tomato paste, and the curry blend, stir together, and cook for about 2 minutes. Add the tomato sauce and heavy cream, raise the heat to medium, and simmer for about 20 minutes, stirring often.

3. Preheat the oven to broil.

4. Mix the yogurt, vegetable oil, garlic, and ginger in a large bowl. Add the chicken chunks to the bowl and coat on all sides with the yogurt mixture. Place the coated chicken pieces on a wire rack inside a shallow baking dish.

5. Broil the chicken for 15 to 20 minutes, turning the chunks over at the halfway point. Transfer the chicken to a serving platter, and strain the juices into the sauce.

6. Add the saffron to the sauce, raise the heat to bring to a strong simmer for 1 to 2 minutes, and pour over the chicken.

CHEF'S TIP

Serve with basmati rice and top with currants, golden raisins, mango chutney, or chopped cashews.

STUFFED CABBAGE WITH LAMB & RICE

SERVES 6 TO 8

CABBAGE
> 1 head green cabbage
> ½ teaspoon salt

SAUCE
> ¼ cup (60 ml) canola or vegetable oil
> 28-ounce (794 g) can crushed tomatoes
> 15-ounce (425 g) can tomato sauce
> 8 tomato Indian Curry Flavor Bombs
> 1 tablespoon (15 ml) ground ginger
> 1 tablespoon (15 ml) curry blend (see Indian Curry Flavor Bomb, page 94)
> Salt, to taste
> Pepper, to taste

STUFFING
> 1 pound (454 g) ground lamb
> 2 cups (330 g) cooked rice
> 2 eggs, beaten
> ¼ cup (30 g) fresh bread crumbs
> 1 tablespoon (15 ml) ground ginger
> 2 tablespoons (8 g) chopped parsley
> 2 teaspoons curry blend (see step 4 of Indian Curry Flavor Bomb, page 94)
> 3 tablespoons (45 ml) prepared sauce (left)
> ½ teaspoon salt
> ¼ teaspoon pepper

1. To prepare the cabbage, trim and core it, discarding any wilted outer leaves.

2. Bring a large pot of water to a boil. Add the salt. Submerge the cabbage head and boil. Using tongs, remove the leaves as they tenderize and fall off the head. Cut off the hard rib end of each leaf and discard. Reserve 1 cup (235 ml) cabbage water.

3. To prepare the sauce, heat the canola or vegetable oil in a large saucepan over medium heat. Add the crushed tomatoes and tomato sauce, using ½ cup (120 ml) reserved cabbage water to pour into the empty cans and get residual tomato juice out. Add the Indian Curry Flavor Bombs, ginger, curry blend, and salt and pepper.

4. Simmer the sauce over medium-low heat for 1 hour and 15 minutes, uncovered, stirring occasionally. Add the remaining ½ cup (120 ml) cabbage water as needed as the sauce reduces. Check and adjust the seasoning.

5. To prepare the stuffing, mix together all of the stuffing ingredients in a large bowl.

6. Preheat the oven to 350°F (180°C, or gas mark 4).

7. Lay out the cabbage leaves on a cutting board, stem end at the bottom. Place 3 to 4 tablespoons (38 to 50 g) of stuffing at the base of each leaf, and then fold in the sides as you roll each leaf up. Keep torn, misshapen, or excess leaves to cover the rolls.

8. Put some sauce in the bottom of a large baking dish. Lay the rolled cabbages, seam side down, in the dish, placing smaller rolls on the inside and larger ones around the outside. Spoon more sauce over the cabbage rolls and cover with set-aside leaves. Cover the baking dish tightly with aluminum foil.

9. Bake the stuffed cabbage rolls for 2 hours. Remove and discard the leaves covering the cabbage rolls. Serve the cabbage rolls with the sauce spooned on top.

MIREPOIX FLAVOR BOMB

MAKES 20 OUNCES (560 G)

- 2 pounds (1 kg) yellow onions
- 1 pound (454 g) carrots (about 8 medium carrots
- 1 pound (454 g) celery (about 11 stalks)
- ½ cup (1 stick/120 g) unsalted butter
- ½ cup (120 ml) extra-virgin olive oil
- ¾ teaspoon salt
- ½ teaspoon pepper

1. Chop the onions, carrots, and celery to approximately ¼-inch (6 mm) dice, either by hand or in a food processor.

2. Heat the butter and olive oil in a large skillet over medium-low heat. Add the onions and cook for approximately 20 minutes.

3. Add the carrots and celery to the skillet with the onions and cook the mixture for an additional 30 to 45 minutes, covered, but stirring often. Add the salt and pepper during the last 15 minutes of cooking. Remove from the heat and set aside.

4. Let the mixture cool, and then spoon it into ice cube trays or small containers and freeze. Once frozen, transfer the Flavor Bombs to an airtight container or a resealable freezer bag.

> **DID YOU KNOW?**
>
> We can thank the chef de cuisine of the Duke of Mirepoix of eighteenth-century France for this essential flavor base of carrots, onions, and celery. We couldn't possibly cook without it!

MIREPOIX FLAVOR BOMB

ROASTED BUTTERNUT SQUASH SOUP

SERVES 4

> 2½ pounds (1.1 kg) cubed butternut squash (about 8 cups)
> ¼ cup (60 ml) water
> 8 Mirepoix Flavor Bombs
> 2 tablespoons (30 ml) extra-virgin olive oil
> ¼ teaspoon salt
> ¼ teaspoon pepper
> 1 large shallot, minced
> 2 tablespoons (30 g) unsalted butter
> 4 cups (950 ml) low-sodium chicken or vegetable broth
> ¼ teaspoon ground nutmeg (optional)
> ¼ teaspoon ground ginger (optional)

1. Preheat the oven to 375°F (190°C, or gas mark 5).

2. Place the butternut squash in a microwave-safe bowl. Sprinkle the squash with the water, cover, and microwave in 4-minute intervals, stirring each time and checking for tenderness. Microwave for up to 12 minutes total.

3. Pour the squash and its liquid into a large roasting pan. Toss with the Mirepoix Flavor Bombs and olive oil and sprinkle with the salt and pepper. Bake in the middle of the oven for about 45 minutes, or until squash is tender when pierced with a fork, stirring at the halfway point. Remove from the oven and let cool.

4. While the squash bakes, sauté the shallot in the butter in a small frying pan over medium-low heat. Cook for about 2 minutes and set aside.

5. When the squash is cool enough to handle, use a food processor to purée it in batches, adding broth with each batch, and adding the sautéed shallot to one of the batches.

6. Pour each batch into a large soup pot and bring to a simmer, stirring often. Cook for 10 minutes. The soup may pop and splatter while cooking; cover with a lid set slightly ajar. Add the nutmeg and ginger, if using, and some additional water or broth if the soup is too thick. Simmer for 5 more minutes.

CHEF'S TIP

To make this soup even more delicious, serve with a sprinkle of grated Parmesan cheese and a swirl of Sage Flavor Bomb oil. To make the oil, blend 1 Sage Flavor Bomb (page 36) with ¼ cup (60 ml) extra-virgin olive oil.

iTALiAN SOFFRiTTO FLAVOR BOMB

MAKES 20 OUNCES (560 G)

- 9 ounces (255 g) garlic (about 3 bulbs), trimmed and peeled
- 1 cup (235 ml) extra-virgin olive oil
- 3 pounds (1.4 kg) yellow onions, trimmed and peeled
- 1 teaspoon salt, divided
- 1 cup (60 g) finely chopped parsley
- 1 cup (60 g) finely chopped basil
- ½ teaspoon pepper

1. Roughly chop the garlic in a food processor. Heat the olive oil in a large frying pan over medium-low heat. Add the garlic and sauté slowly, about 15 minutes, until lightly golden.

2. Roughly chop the onions in a food processor. Add to the pan with the garlic and cook for about 30 minutes, covered, stirring occasionally. Uncover, add ½ teaspoon salt, and cook for an additional 30 minutes, stirring often.

3. Add the chopped herbs to the pan and stir to blend. Add the remaining ½ teaspoon salt and the pepper. Remove from the heat and set aside.

4. Let the mixture cool, and then spoon it into ice cube trays or small containers, or onto a wax paper–lined baking sheet or tray, and freeze. Once frozen, transfer the Flavor Bombs to an airtight container or a resealable freezer bag.

TURKEY MEATLOAF OR MEATBALLS

MEATLOAF SERVES 4 OR MAKES 10 TO 12 MEATBALLS

- 1¼ pounds (570 g) ground turkey
- 2 cups (120 g) fresh bread crumbs, plus more if needed
- 1 egg
- ¼ cup (25 g) grated Parmesan or Pecorino Romano cheese
- ¼ cup (60 g) tomato sauce
- 2 tablespoons (30 ml) fat-free half-and-half or milk
- 2 tablespoons (30 ml) extra-virgin olive oil
- 4 Italian Soffritto Flavor Bombs
- ½ teaspoon salt
- ½ teaspoon pepper

CONTINUED > > >

1. Preheat the oven to 350°F (180°C, or gas mark 4).

2. Mix all the ingredients together in a large bowl. Do not overwork; keep the mixture fluffy. Add more bread crumbs if the mixture is too soft.

3. Shape the meatloaf mixture into a football in a baking dish. Push in the ends to square it off a bit, so it is uniform for cooking.

4. Bake the meatloaf, uncovered, for about 40 minutes, or until the internal temperature reaches 160°F (71°C). Let it rest for 10 minutes, so the juices in the pan are absorbed. Slice and serve the meatloaf.

RECIPE VARIATION

To make meatballs, after step 2, shape the mixture into 10 to 12 balls and fry in ½ cup (120 ml) extra-virgin olive oil. Turn the meatballs often to brown on all sides—use two spoons for an easy way to turn the meatballs.

iTALiAN SOFFRiTTO FLAVOR BOMB
MEMA'S VEAL STEW

SERVES 4

- 2 pounds (1 kg) veal stew meat, cut into chunks
- ½ cup (60 g) seasoned flour (see Chef's Tip, page 74)
- 2 tablespoons (30 ml) extra-virgin olive oil
- 2 tablespoons (30 g) unsalted butter
- 6 Italian Soffritto Flavor Bombs
- 1 tablespoon (16 g) tomato paste
- 1 cup (235 ml) low-sodium beef broth or water, divided
- 15-ounce (425 g) can tomato sauce
- 2 medium carrots
- 15-ounce (425 g) can peas with liquid (or fresh or frozen)
- 3 small Yukon Gold potatoes, peeled and diced (optional)
- Salt, to taste
- Pepper, to taste

1. Dredge the veal in the seasoned flour. Heat the olive oil and butter in a large skillet or Dutch oven over medium heat until shimmering. Add the veal and brown on all sides, about 10 minutes. The veal will release juices that will help create the gravy.

2. Add the Italian Soffritto Flavor Bombs and tomato paste to the skillet and stir, scraping up any stuck-on flour to thicken the liquid. Add about ½ cup (120 ml) beef broth and continue stirring. Add the tomato sauce and remaining ½ cup (120 ml) broth, if needed to cover the veal.

3. Reduce the heat to low and simmer for 1 hour, uncovered, stirring often.

4. Peel and slice the carrots. Put in a microwave-safe bowl with a sprinkle of water, cover, and microwave for about 5 minutes. (If using fresh or frozen peas, microwave them with the carrots and add an extra 3 minutes to the microwave time. If using potatoes, microwave them with the peas and carrots, and add an extra 5 minutes to the microwave time.)

5. Add the carrots, peas, and potatoes (if using) to the skillet with the veal. The gravy should be fairly thick; if the sauce is thin, do not add the liquid from the can of peas. Simmer, stirring often, for at least 30 minutes more, until the veal is very tender. Season to taste with salt and pepper.

> **CHEF'S TiP**
>
> You can choose to add the potatoes or not. Mema made mashed potatoes on the side, which was heavenly.

iTALiAN SOFFRiTTO FLAVOR BOMB
STUFFED PEPPERS & ZUCCHiNi SERVES 6 TO 8

- 4 large red peppers
- 4 medium zucchini
- ½ pound (225 g) Italian sausage (removed from casing)
- ½ cup (120 ml) extra-virgin olive oil, plus more for drizzling
- 1 tablespoon (16 g) tomato paste
- 6 Italian Soffritto Flavor Bombs
- 2 cups (490 g) crushed tomatoes or tomato sauce, divided
- 2 to 3 cups (120 to 180 g) fresh bread crumbs
- ⅓ cup (40 g) grated Parmesan or Pecorino Romano cheese
- 2 tablespoons (18 g) pignoli (pine nuts, optional)
- 1 tablespoon (6 g) chopped pitted oil-cured olives (optional)
- 1 tablespoon (9 g) golden raisins (optional)
- ¾ cup (90 g) shredded mozzarella

1. Slice the peppers in half lengthwise and remove the stems and seeds. Microwave the peppers in a microwave-safe dish with a sprinkle of water for 5 minutes.

2. Trim the zucchini and slice them in half lengthwise. (You can also cut them in half widthwise, if necessary to fit in the baking dish.) Microwave the zucchini in a microwave-safe dish with a sprinkle of water for 5 minutes. Let cool. When zucchini are cool enough to handle, scoop out the flesh using a melon baller. Chop the flesh and set aside.

3. In a large frying pan over medium heat, cook the sausage, breaking it into small pieces, for about 10 minutes. Add the chopped zucchini flesh and sauté for 5 minutes.

4. Add the olive oil, tomato paste, and Italian Soffritto Flavor Bombs to the pan, and blend into the sausage-zucchini mixture. Add 1 cup (245 g) crushed tomatoes or sauce, and simmer for 10 minutes, stirring often.

5. Add 2 cups (120 g) bread crumbs. If the filling mixture seems too wet, add up to 1 cup (60 g) more. Remove the mixture from the heat and let it cool a bit. Stir in the grated Parmesan. Add the pignoli, olives, and raisins (if using) to the filling.

6. Preheat the oven to 350°F (180°C, or gas mark 4). Grease a baking dish.

7. Fill the zucchini and peppers with 2 to 3 tablespoons (25 to 37 g) of filling each. Place the stuffed vegetables in the baking dish and sprinkle with the shredded mozzarella. Spoon the remaining 1 cup (245 g) tomatoes over the stuffed vegetables, and drizzle with some oil.

8. Cover the baking dish tightly with aluminum foil. Bake for about 45 minutes, or until bubbling.

BEEF STOCK
FLAVOR BOMB

STOCK & SAUCE
FLAVOR BOMBS

BÉCHAMEL
FLAVOR BOMB

VEGETABLE STOCK
FLAVOR BOMB

CHICKEN STOCK
FLAVOR BOMB

BÉCHAMEL FLAVOR BOMB

MAKES 24 OUNCES (672 G)

- ½ cup (1 stick/120 g) unsalted butter
- 1 cup (120 g) seasoned flour (see Chef's Tip, page 74)
- 2 cups (475 ml) milk (I use 1%), plus additional if necessary
- 1 cup (235 ml) fat-free half-and-half
- ½ teaspoon ground nutmeg
- Salt, to taste
- Pepper, to taste

1. Melt the butter in a 3-quart (2.8 L) saucepan over medium heat. Add the flour to the saucepan and whisk, cooking and stirring for about 3 minutes.

2. Add the milk and half-and-half, 1 cup (235 ml) at a time, whisking constantly until all the liquid is incorporated. Lower the heat and simmer, continually stirring, for 3 to 5 more minutes. If the sauce seems too thick, add more milk as necessary.

3. Add the nutmeg to the mixture and stir. Taste for salt and pepper, and adjust if needed. Remove from the heat and set aside.

4. Let the mixture cool, and then spoon it into ice cube trays or small containers and freeze. Once frozen, transfer the Flavor Bombs to an airtight container or a resealable freezer bag.

BÉCHAMEL FLAVOR BOMB
POTATO LEEK GRATIN

SERVES 4

- ½ pound (225 g) leeks (about 3 leeks)
- 3 Vegetable Stock Flavor Bombs (page 138) or 6 tablespoons (90 ml) store-bought vegetable stock
- 1 tablespoon (15 g) unsalted butter
- ¼ cup (60 ml) water
- ¼ teaspoon salt
- ¼ teaspoon pepper
- 1 pound (454 g) Yukon Gold potatoes, peeled and thinly sliced (use a mandoline, if possible)
- Cheese Sauce (page 120), made using only 2 tablespoons (30 ml) half-and-half or milk
- Milk, as needed
- 2 to 3 tablespoons (8 to 12 g) fresh bread crumbs

1. Remove and discard the outer leaves of the leeks, slice the leeks into ½-inch (13 mm) rings, and soak in a large bowl of water to remove all of the dirt. Drain and rinse as needed.

2. In a medium skillet over medium heat, heat the Vegetable Stock Flavor Bombs, butter, and water until sizzling. Add the leeks and bring to a simmer over medium heat, and then braise for about 15 minutes. Taste for salt and pepper, and adjust if needed.

3. Remove the leeks from the skillet with a slotted spoon or spatula. Transfer to a bowl, and then squeeze all liquid from the leeks into the skillet. Set the leeks aside.

4. Add the potatoes to the skillet, coating them with the braising liquid. Cover the skillet and let the potatoes cook for about 5 minutes, over low heat, stirring occasionally. Add a bit more water if necessary.

5. Preheat the oven to 375°F (190°C, or gas mark 5). Grease a 9-inch (23 cm) round or square baking dish.

6. Starting with the potatoes, make layers of potatoes, leeks, and cheese sauce in the baking dish. End with potatoes on top, and reserve some cheese sauce.

7. Thin the remaining cheese sauce with a little milk, and then pour over top. Sprinkle the gratin with the bread crumbs.

8. Cover the gratin with aluminum foil and bake for 40 minutes. Remove the foil and bake for 20 minutes more, until golden brown and bubbling. Let the gratin rest for about 10 minutes before serving.

CHEF'S TIP

Use this recipe for other vegetable gratins, too.

BÉCHAMEL FLAVOR BOMB
CHEESE SAUCE SERVES 4

> - 3 Béchamel Flavor Bombs
> - 4 ounces (115 g) shredded Cheddar, Fontina, or Gruyère cheese
> - 3 to 4 tablespoons (45 to 60 ml) fat-free half-and-half or low-fat milk

1. In a small saucepan over medium-low heat, melt the Béchamel Flavor Bombs.

2. Add the cheese, whisking constantly, and then add the half-and-half or milk, whisking constantly, until the cheese melts and the sauce becomes smooth.

3. Cook until the sauce just starts to simmer or to your preferred thickness.

CHEF'S TIP

Pour this over any vegetable, or use it in gratins, casseroles, and macaroni and cheese.

BÉCHAMEL FLAVOR BOMB

SHRIMP TARTLETS
MAKES 45

- > ¾ pound (340 g) shrimp, peeled and deveined (any size)
- > ½ teaspoon garlic powder
- > 1 tablespoon (15 ml) extra-virgin olive oil
- > ¼ cup (½ stick/60 g) unsalted butter
- > 1 large shallot, minced
- > 1¾ cups (170 g) white button mushrooms or 4 Umami Flavor Bombs (page 70)
- > 3 tablespoons (45 ml) sherry
- > 1 tablespoon (15 ml) soy sauce
- > 6 Béchamel Flavor Bombs
- > Salt, to taste
- > Pepper, to taste
- > ¾ cup (90 g) shredded Gruyère cheese
- > 45 frozen mini phyllo (or filo or fillo) shells

1. Rinse and dry the shrimp. Freeze them for about 20 minutes (slightly frozen shrimp are easier to chop).

2. Chop the slightly frozen shrimp into bite-size pieces. Sprinkle them with the garlic powder and olive oil and set aside.

3. Heat the butter in a medium saucepan over medium-low heat until sizzling, and then sauté the shallot for 2 to 3 minutes.

4. If using fresh mushrooms (instead of the Umami Flavor Bombs), rinse, dry, and finely chop them. Add the mushrooms to the pan with the shallots, and cook over medium-high heat until browned and any liquid released by the mushrooms is absorbed, about 5 minutes. If using fresh mushrooms, then add the sherry and soy sauce to the pan with the mushrooms and simmer. Remove the mushrooms and shallots from the pan, and set aside.

5. Add the shrimp to the pan and sauté over medium heat until pink, 3 to 5 minutes. (Shallots will still be in the pan if using the Umami Flavor Bombs.)

6. Add the Umami Flavor Bombs (if using), sherry, and soy sauce (if not added with fresh mushrooms), and simmer for about 2 minutes. If fresh mushrooms were used, return the mushroom-shallot mixture to the pan with the shrimp.

7. Add the Béchamel Flavor Bombs and stir to blend. Taste for salt and pepper, and adjust if needed. Remove the pan from the heat and let cool.

8. If baking the tartlets immediately, preheat the oven to 400°F (200°C, or gas mark 6).

9. When the shrimp mixture has cooled, add the Gruyère and stir to blend. Spoon the shrimp mixture into the phyllo shells. You can freeze them for later baking (carefully peel back the cellophane and place back in the box) or, to prepare immediately, place the filled shells on an ungreased baking sheet and bake for about 5 minutes, or until bubbling and slightly golden brown.

BÉCHAMEL FLAVOR BOMB

SAUSAGE GRAVY SERVES 2 TO 4

> 4 pork, turkey, or chicken sausage links or ½ pound (225 g) Italian or country sausage (removed from casing)
> 4 Béchamel Flavor Bombs
> ½ cup (120 ml) fat-free half-and-half, heavy cream, or whole milk
> ¼ teaspoon ground nutmeg
> Pepper, to taste

1. In a medium nonstick skillet over medium-high heat, cook the sausage until cooked through and browned, about 7 minutes.

2. Add the Béchamel Flavor Bombs to the skillet, mixing with the sausage meat. Add the half-and-half (or cream or milk) and simmer for about 2 minutes, stirring often, until thick and bubbling. Add the nutmeg and pepper, and stir.

3. Serve with Flaky Buttermilk Biscuits (see recipe below).

FLAKY BUTTERMILK BISCUITS MAKES 10

> 2 cups (250 g) all-purpose unbleached flour
> 2 teaspoons baking powder
> 1¼ teaspoons salt
> ½ teaspoon baking soda
> 12 tablespoons (1½ sticks/ 180 g) very cold unsalted butter, cut into cubes, or 8 tablespoons (1 stick/120 g) unsalted butter and 4 Beef Stock Bombs (page 124)
> ¾ cup (175 ml) very cold buttermilk
> 1 egg, beaten

1. Pulse the flour, baking powder, salt, and baking soda in a food processor. Add the butter and pulse a few times, until the mixture has a coarse texture, with pea-size bits of butter.

2. Pour the mixture into a large bowl, and sprinkle the buttermilk all around the flour. Mix it in with a spatula until a shaggy dough forms.

3. Turn the dough out onto a lightly floured countertop. Knead lightly and quickly to form the dough, and then pat it to about 1½ inches (4 cm) thick.

4. Cut out biscuits with a 3-inch (7.5 cm) biscuit cutter, pushing straight down (not twisting the cutter). You should have about 10 biscuits.

5. Place the biscuits on a baking sheet and refrigerate for about 30 minutes.

6. Preheat the oven to 375°F (190°C, or gas mark 5). Brush the tops with the beaten egg. Bake for 30 to 35 minutes, or until golden brown and risen.

BEEF STOCK FLAVOR BOMB

MAKES 48 OUNCES (1.3 KG)

- > 2 pounds (1 kg) beef chuck neck bones
- > 1 pound (454 g) lamb bones for stew or veal bones
- > 1 yellow onion, unpeeled and cut in half
- > 2 medium carrots, peeled and cut into quarters
- > 2 celery stalks, cut into quarters
- > 1 tablespoon (15 ml) vegetable oil
- > 4 quarts (1 gallon/3.8 L) water
- > 1 cup (235 ml) hot water
- > 2 bay leaves
- > 1 whole clove
- > 1 tablespoon (15 ml) whole peppercorns
- > ½ teaspoon salt
- > 1 sprig of thyme or rosemary

1. Preheat the oven to 300°F (150°C, or gas mark 2).

2. Place the bones, onion, carrots, and celery in a baking dish, and toss with the vegetable oil. Place in the oven and roast for 1 hour.

3. Remove the bones and vegetables from the oven and transfer to a large stockpot. Cover with the 4 quarts (3.8 L) water. Deglaze the baking pan with the 1 cup (235 ml) hot water and add the liquid to the stockpot.

4. Add the bay leaves, clove, peppercorns, salt, and thyme or rosemary to the stockpot, and bring to a simmer. Keep the stock at a low simmer, uncovered, for at least 6 hours.

5. Strain the stock through a mesh strainer and squeeze the liquid out of the solids when cool enough to handle. Set aside. Dispose of the solids.

6. Let the stock cool, and then refrigerate until fat solidifies at the top. Peel off the fat and freeze for future use in pie crusts (page 69) and biscuits (page 122).

7. The stock will be gelled, so lightly heat it to a consistency to spoon it into ice cube trays or small containers and freeze. Once frozen, transfer the Flavor Bombs to an airtight container or a resealable freezer bag.

BEEF STOCK FLAVOR BOMB

SIRLOIN STEAKS WITH COGNAC PAN SAUCE SERVES 2

> 2 sirloin steaks (10 ounces/ 284 g each), about 1 inch (2.5 cm) thick
> ¼ teaspoon salt, plus more to taste
> ¼ teaspoon pepper, plus more to taste
> 1 tablespoon (15 g) unsalted butter
> 2 tablespoons (20 g) minced shallot (about 1 small shallot)
> 1 tablespoon (15 ml) all-purpose unbleached flour
> ¼ cup (60 ml) cognac
> 3 Beef Stock Flavor Bombs

1. Preheat the oven to 300°F (150°C, or gas mark 2).

2. Place a wire rack in a shallow baking dish. Sprinkle the steaks with salt and pepper and place on the rack. Cook in the oven for 20 minutes. Remove the steaks from the oven.

3. Heat the butter in a medium frying pan over medium-high heat until sizzling. Add the steaks, searing for about 3 minutes on each side. Remove the steaks from the frying pan and keep warm in an oven heated at a low temperature.

4. Add the shallot to the pan and sauté for 2 minutes over medium heat. Add the flour and whisk for about 2 minutes to make a roux. Add the cognac, whisk, and simmer to reduce, about 2 minutes. Add the Beef Stock Flavor Bombs, whisk, and simmer for about 1 minute. Taste for salt and pepper, and adjust if needed.

5. Pour the sauce over the steaks and serve immediately.

CHEF'S TIP

Cooking the steaks in a low oven before searing is a great method that eliminates the overcooked edges that often result from searing.

BEEF STOCK FLAVOR BOMB

FILET MIGNON WITH RED WINE REDUCTION SERVES 2

> 2 filet mignon steaks
  (6 ounces/170 g each)
> ¼ teaspoon salt, plus more
  to taste
> ¼ teaspoon pepper, plus more
  to taste
> 1 tablespoon (15 g) unsalted
  butter
> 2 tablespoons (20 g) minced
  shallot (about 1 small shallot)
> ¼ cup (60 ml) red wine
  (such as Pinot Noir, Chianti,
  or Cabernet)
> 3 Beef Stock Flavor Bombs

1. Preheat the oven to 300°F (150°C, or gas mark 2).

2. Sprinkle the steaks with salt and pepper. Heat the butter in a medium frying pan over medium-high heat until sizzling, then sear the steaks on both sides, about 1 minute per side.

3. If your frying pan is ovenproof, place it directly in the oven; otherwise, transfer the steaks to a baking dish and place in the oven. Cook the steaks for 15 minutes for medium-rare. (Cook longer if you prefer steaks more well done.) Remove the steaks from the oven and baking dish and keep warm on a plate that has been warmed in the microwave for a minute.

4. Add the shallot to the frying pan that the steaks were in and sauté for 2 minutes over medium heat. Add the wine and simmer to reduce, 1 to 2 minutes. Add the Beef Stock Flavor Bombs and simmer for 1 minute. Taste for salt and pepper, and adjust if needed.

5. Pour the pan sauce over the steaks and serve immediately. The steaks will have rested perfectly while the sauce was prepared.

BEEF STOCK FLAVOR BOMB

BEEF BOURGUIGNON

SERVES 4

- › 2 pounds (1 kg) boneless beef chuck roast
- › ¼ teaspoon salt
- › ¼ teaspoon pepper
- › 1 tablespoon (15 ml) vegetable oil or bacon fat
- › 6 Beef Stock Flavor Bombs
- › 6 Suppengrün Flavor Bombs (page 62) or Mirepoix Flavor Bombs (page 102) or 1 medium carrot, 1 celery stalk, and 1 small onion, diced and sautéed
- › 1 tablespoon (16 g) tomato paste
- › 1 tablespoon (16 g) miso paste or 1 tablespoon (15 ml) soy sauce
- › 2 bay leaves
- › 1 tablespoon (4 g) chopped fresh or ½ tablespoon (7.5 ml) dried rosemary
- › 2 cups (475 ml) red wine (such as Pinot Noir or Chianti; don't use a very strong wine, as it will overpower the dish)
- › ¼ cup (60 ml) water

1. Preheat the oven to 300°F (150°C, or gas mark 2).

2. Trim the beef of fat and cut it into 2-inch (5 cm) chunks. Sprinkle the beef with salt and pepper.

3. Heat the vegetable oil or bacon fat in a large Dutch oven over medium to medium-high heat until shimmering. Sear the beef chunks until browned on all sides, 8 to 10 minutes. Use a pot large enough that you can sear the beef in a single layer (so it does not steam), or sear in two batches. You want to build a fond (a browned layer) in the bottom of the pot.

4. Add the Beef Stock Flavor Bombs, the Suppengrün or Mirepoix Flavor Bombs (or the vegetables), the tomato paste, and the miso or soy sauce to the Dutch oven. Deglaze the pot and stir, simmering for 2 minutes over medium heat.

5. Add the bay leaves and rosemary to the Dutch oven and stir. Add the wine and simmer for 2 minutes. Add the water and stir.

6. Cover the Dutch oven with its lid and place in the oven. Cook the beef for 2 hours, stirring halfway through. Remove the bay leaves and rosemary sprigs. Serve immediately.

CHEF'S TIP

It is always best to use whole roasts rather than precut chunks. When you trim and cut the chuck roast yourself, you are guaranteed that the chunks are all from the same cut of meat.

CHiCKEN STOCK FLAVOR BOMB

MAKES 40 OUNCES (1.1 KG)

> - 4 pounds (1.8 kg) dark meat chicken (6 wings, 4 thighs, 4 legs and/or backs)
> - 3 quarts (2.8 L) water
> - 1 medium carrot, peeled and cut into quarters
> - 1 celery stalk, cut into quarters
> - 1 medium yellow onion, unpeeled and cut into quarters
> - 2 bay leaves
> - 1 tablespoon (15 ml) salt

1. Put the chicken in a large stockpot and cover with the 3 quarts (2.8 L) water. Bring ALMOST to a boil.

2. Lower the heat and simmer for 2 to 3 hours, skimming any foam off the top.

3. Add the carrot, celery, onion, bay leaves, and salt to the stockpot, and continue simmering for 3 more hours.

4. Strain the stock through a mesh strainer and squeeze the liquid out of the solids when cool enough to handle. Set aside. Dispose of the solids, though there may be some salvageable chicken pieces to separate, but most of it will be cooked out and have fallen apart.

5. Let the stock cool, and then refrigerate until the fat solidifies at the top; scoop off the "schmaltz" and freeze for future use for frying or in matzo balls.

6. The stock will be gelled, so lightly heat it to a consistency to spoon it into ice cube trays or small containers and freeze. Once frozen, transfer the Flavor Bombs to an airtight container or a resealable freezer bag.

STRACCiATELLA (ROMAN EGG DROP SOUP)

SERVES 2

- > **4 eggs**
- > **¼ teaspoon ground nutmeg**
- > **¾ cup (90 g) grated Parmesan cheese**
- > **2 tablespoons (30 ml) fresh lemon juice**
- > **2 tablespoons (8 g) minced fresh parsley**
- > **½ teaspoon salt**
- > **12 Chicken Stock Flavor Bombs**
- > **1 cup (235 ml) water**
- > **Pepper (optional)**
- > **Extra-virgin olive oil (optional)**

1. Beat the eggs in a small bowl until just blended.

2. Mix the nutmeg into the grated cheese, then blend into the eggs. Add the lemon juice, parsley, and salt.

3. In a large pot, bring the Chicken Stock Flavor Bombs and water to a rolling boil. Pour in the egg mixture gradually, in a thin stream through a wire whisk, creating ribbons. Stir with the whisk. Cook for 1 to 2 minutes, or until the egg is cooked through.

4. Sprinkle with pepper and drizzle with olive oil (if using). Serve immediately.

CHEF'S TiP

This soup is traditionally made with chicken stock, but it's also delicious with beef or vegetable stock or a combination of stocks.

CHICKEN STOCK FLAVOR BOMB

CHICKEN & DUMPLINGS SERVES 4

CHICKEN STEW

> 1½ pounds (680 g) chicken thighs, skin removed
> ¼ cup (30 g) seasoned flour (see Chef's Tip, page 74)
> 2 tablespoons unsalted butter (30 g), vegetable oil (30 ml), or schmaltz (26 g)
> 4 Mirepoix Flavor Bombs (page 102)
> 8 Chicken Stock Flavor Bombs
> 6 cups (1.5 L) water or low-sodium chicken broth
> Salt, to taste
> Pepper, to taste

DUMPLINGS

> 1 cup (120 g) all-purpose unbleached flour
> ¼ teaspoon baking soda
> ½ teaspoon salt
> ⅓ cup (80 ml) cold buttermilk
> 2 tablespoons (30 g) unsalted butter, melted and cooled
> 1 large egg white

1. To make the chicken stew, dredge the chicken thighs in the seasoned flour.

2. In a large Dutch oven over medium to medium-high heat, heat the butter, vegetable oil, or schmaltz until shimmering. Sear the chicken for about 5 minutes on each side.

3. Add the Mirepoix Flavor Bombs and stir. (You can substitute 2 carrots, 2 celery stalks, and 1 small onion, all diced, for the Mirepoix Flavor Bomb. Sauté with the chicken for about 8 minutes, until caramelized.) Add the Chicken Stock Flavor Bombs and the water or chicken broth. Bring just to a boil, then lower the heat and simmer the stew for at least 1 hour.

4. Remove the chicken from the stew, let it cool, and break it into pieces (by hand or with scissors). Set aside. Skim the fat from the settled broth if necessary, and return the chicken to the pot.

5. To make the dumplings, whisk together the flour, baking soda, and salt in a large bowl.

6. Combine the buttermilk and melted butter in a separate bowl, stirring until the butter forms clumps. Whisk in the egg white.

7. Add the buttermilk mixture to the flour mixture. Stir with a spatula until blended and a dough forms. Do not overmix.

8. Bring the chicken stew back to a simmer. Taste for salt and pepper, and adjust if needed. Drop the dumpling dough by the tablespoon (15 g) over the top of the stew, keeping the dumplings about ¼ inch (6 mm) apart from each other. The dough should make 10 to 12 dumplings.

9. Cover the stew and simmer gently until the dumplings have doubled in size, about 15 minutes. Serve immediately.

CHICKEN PICCATA SERVES 3

- › 6 boneless, skinless chicken breasts (6 ounces/170 g each)
- › ⅓ cup (40 g) seasoned flour (see Chef's Tip, page 74)
- › ¼ cup (52 g) schmaltz (optional)
- › ¼ cup unsalted butter (½ stick/60 g) or vegetable oil (60 ml)
- › 1 tablespoon (10 g) minced shallot (optional)
- › ¼ cup (60 ml) dry white wine (such as Pinot Grigio, Chardonnay, or Frascati)
- › 3 Chicken Stock Flavor Bombs
- › 3 tablespoons (45 ml) lemon juice
- › 2 tablespoons (18 g) capers

1. Trim, rinse, and pat dry the chicken breasts. They can be sliced thin or pounded into cutlets. Dredge the cutlets in the seasoned flour.

2. Heat the schmaltz, if using, and butter or vegetable oil in a medium frying pan over medium heat until shimmering. Working in batches, fry the cutlets for 3 to 4 minutes on each side, until golden brown. Remove the cutlets to a serving dish. Cover and keep warm in an oven at low heat.

3. Add the shallot to the pan and sauté, stirring, over low heat for 2 minutes.

4. Add the wine to the pan and deglaze, simmering for about 2 minutes. Add the Chicken Stock Flavor Bombs, lemon juice, and capers. Simmer for 2 to 3 minutes, until the sauce thickens a bit. Return the cutlets to the pan and coat with the sauce. Serve immediately.

CHEF'S TIP

If you don't have the shallot, it won't be seriously missed. The capers and lemon offer fabulous flavor on their own.

CHICKEN STOCK FLAVOR BOMB

CHICKEN CUTLETS WITH SUPPENGRÜN PAN SAUCE SERVES 3 TO 4

> - 6 boneless, skinless chicken breasts (6 ounces/170 g each)
> - ⅓ cup (40 g) seasoned flour (see Chef's Tip, page 74)
> - ¼ cup (52 g) schmaltz (optional)
> - ¼ cup unsalted butter (½ stick/60 g) or vegetable oil (60 ml)
> - 3 Chicken Stock Flavor Bombs
> - 1 teaspoon miso paste
> - Salt, to taste
> - Pepper, to taste
> - 6 Suppengrün Flavor Bombs

1. Trim, rinse, and pat dry the chicken breasts. They can be sliced thin or pounded into cutlets. Dredge the cutlets in the seasoned flour.

2. Heat the schmaltz, if using, and butter or vegetable oil in a medium frying pan over medium heat until shimmering. Working in batches, fry the cutlets for 3 to 4 minutes on each side, until golden brown. Remove the cutlets to a serving dish and keep warm.

3. Let the pan cool a bit. Then add the Chicken Stock Flavor Bombs and miso paste. Simmer for 2 minutes. Taste for salt and pepper, and adjust if needed. Water or stock can be added if the sauce is too salty.

4. Add the Suppengrün Flavor Bombs (or Bombs of your choice; see Note) and simmer for 2 minutes. Pour the sauce over the chicken cutlets and serve.

RECIPE VARIATION

For a different flavor, substitute 6 of any of the other Vegetable-Blend Flavor Bombs (page 60) for the Suppengrün Flavor Bombs. You can also substitute any of the Herb Pesto Flavor Bombs (page 20), but in that case, use only 2, as the flavors are more potent.

VEGETABLE STOCK
FLAVOR BOMB
MAKES 48 OUNCES (1.3 KG)

> 5 medium carrots, peeled
> 2 russet potatoes, peeled
> 1 turnip, peeled
> 1 knob celery root, peeled
> 2 leeks
> 1 medium yellow onion, unpeeled and cut in half
> ¼ cup (60 ml) water plus 4 quarts (1 gallon/3.8 L) water, divided
> Small bunch of parsley
> 2 bay leaves
> 2 tablespoons (5 g) fresh thyme or 1 tablespoon (15 ml) dried thyme
> 1 tablespoon (16 g) tomato paste
> 1 tablespoon (16 g) miso paste
> 1 tablespoon (15 ml) whole peppercorns

1. Chop the carrots, potatoes, turnip, and celery root into 2-inch (5 cm) pieces.

2. Remove and discard the outer leaves of the leeks, slice the leeks into large disks, and soak them in a large bowl of water to remove all of the dirt. Drain and rinse if needed.

3. In a large stockpot over low heat, sweat the vegetables (carrots, potatoes, turnip, celery root, leeks, and onion) in the ¼ cup (60 ml) of water, covering and uncovering, until fond (a browned layer) starts to form on the bottom of the stockpot, approximately 20 minutes

4. Add the parsley, bay leaves, thyme, tomato paste, miso paste, and peppercorns to the stockpot, and stir.

5. Cover with the remaining 4 quarts (3.8 L) water and bring just to a boil. Lower the heat and simmer, uncovered, for 3½ hours.

6. Strain the stock through a mesh strainer and squeeze the liquid out of the solids when cool enough to handle. Set aside. Dispose of the solids.

7. Let the stock cool, and then spoon it into ice cube trays or small containers and freeze. Once frozen, transfer the Flavor Bombs to an airtight container or a resealable freezer bag.

VEGETABLE STOCK FLAVOR BOMB

MALFATTI GNOCCHI WiTH VEGETABLE STOCK GLAZE SERVES 4

- › **5 cups (1.2 L) salted water**
- › **12 Malfatti Gnocchi (page 142)**
- › **2 tablespoons (30 g) unsalted butter**
- › **3 Vegetable Stock Flavor Bombs**
- › **1 Sage Flavor Bomb (page 36) or 1 tablespoon (2 g) minced fresh sage and 1 tablespoon (10 g) minced sautéed shallot**
- › **Salt, to taste**
- › **Pepper, to taste**
- › **Grated Parmesan cheese, to taste**
- › **Extra-virgin olive oil (optional)**

1. In a medium pot, bring the water to a boil. Boil the gnocchi for 7 to 8 minutes, or until they float to the top and are somewhat firm.

2. Remove the gnocchi from the water with a slotted spoon. Transfer to a serving dish, cover, and keep warm in an oven at low heat.

3. Discard all but 2 cups (475 ml) pasta water. Reduce to about 1 cup (235 ml) by boiling over medium-high heat for about 5 minutes.

4. Add the butter, Vegetable Stock Flavor Bombs, and Sage Flavor Bomb to the pot and simmer. Taste for salt and pepper, and adjust if needed.

5. Pour the glaze over the gnocchi. Sprinkle with grated Parmesan cheese, drizzle with olive oil (if using), and serve immediately.

CONTINUED > > >

MALFATTI GNOCCHI SERVES 4

- 1 pound (454 g) part-skim ricotta
- 10-ounce (280 g) package frozen chopped spinach, defrosted
- 3 large eggs
- 1 cup (120 g) grated Parmesan or Pecorino Romano cheese
- 2 tablespoons (30 g) mascarpone cheese or 3 Béchamel Flavor Bombs (page 116)
- ½ cup (1 stick/120 g) unsalted butter, melted and cooled
- 1 teaspoon salt
- ¼ teaspoon freshly cracked black pepper
- ½ cup (60 g) seasoned unbleached all-purpose flour (seasoned with salt, pepper, and garlic powder), plus more for shaping

DID YOU KNOW?

Malfatti means "poorly made" in Italian.

1. Line a large bowl with paper towels and cheesecloth. Spoon the ricotta into the cheesecloth and wrap tightly, twisting the ends. Squeeze out and discard the liquid, and place the ricotta in the bowl.

2. Use the same method to squeeze out the chopped spinach. Mix the spinach with the ricotta.

3. Beat the eggs in a small bowl. Add the eggs to the ricotta and spinach and stir. Add the grated cheese, mascarpone or Béchamel Flavor Bombs, butter, salt, pepper, and flour, and blend.

4. Put a teaspoon of flour into a wine glass and drop in a heaping tablespoon of ricotta mixture. Swirl the glass until an oval shape forms. (You may need to quickly shake the glass back and forth to create an egg shape.)

5. Drop the dumpling out onto a tray. Repeat to form more dumplings, reflouring the glass as needed. (You should get about 30 dumplings.) The dumplings can be frozen at this point.

6. To cook the dumplings, bring about 6 cups (1.4 L) salted water to a boil, drop in the malfatti a few at a time, and cook for about 8 minutes (they will float when they're done).

7. Remove the malfatti with a slotted spoon. Transfer to a serving dish and cover to keep warm.

8. Serve with Vegetable Stock Glaze (page 141), Béchamel Sauce (page 74), or marinara sauce.

BRAiSED BOK CHOY

SERVES 4

- › 2 pounds (1 kg) bok choy (about 6 heads)
- › 9 Vegetable Stock Flavor Bombs
- › 3 tablespoons unsalted butter (42 g) or extra-virgin olive oil (45 ml)
- › Salt, to taste
- › Pepper, to taste

1. Trim the ends of the bok choy heads and cut in half lengthwise. Soak and clean the bok choy well, rinsing between leaves to remove hidden dirt.

2. In a large skillet, bring the Vegetable Stock Flavor Bombs and butter or olive oil to a simmer over medium-high heat. Add the bok choy, lower the heat, cover, and simmer for 10 minutes. Using tongs, turn the bok choy to the other side, cover, and simmer for 10 more minutes. Transfer the bok choy to a serving platter. Cover and keep warm in an oven at low heat.

3. Return the braising broth to a rapid simmer for 2 to 3 minutes to reduce to a glaze-like consistency. Taste for salt and pepper, and adjust if needed. If the broth is too salty, add some water and slightly reduce again. Pour the broth over the bok choy and serve.

iTALiAN-STYLE BAKED ESCAROLE SERVES 4

- 1 head escarole
- 5 tablespoons (75 ml) extra-virgin olive oil, plus more for drizzling
- 4 Italian Soffritto Flavor Bombs (page 106)
- 9 Vegetable Stock Flavor Bombs
- ¼ teaspoon salt
- ¼ teaspoon pepper
- ¼ cup (60 ml) water
- 2 tablespoons (12 g) roughly chopped pitted olives (Kalamata or oil-cured black)
- 1 tablespoon (9 g) capers, drained
- 2 tablespoons (18 g) golden raisins
- 1½ tablespoons (14 g) pignoli (pine nuts)
- 2 tablespoons (14 g) grated Pecorino Romano or Parmesan, divided
- 3 tablespoons (12 g) fresh bread crumbs or panko

1. Preheat the oven to 350°F (180°C, or gas mark 4).

2. Trim a slice off the stem end of the escarole, but leave the core intact. Remove the wilted outer leaves. Cut the escarole in half lengthwise and then into quarters. Soak the escarole in a large bowl of water, and rinse twice to remove all grit.

3. In a large skillet over medium-high heat, combine the olive oil, Italian Soffritto Flavor Bombs, and Vegetable Stock Flavor Bombs. Bring to a simmer.

4. Add the escarole to the skillet and simmer for 3 minutes. Turn the escarole wedges over with tongs, coating with the braising liquid. Add the salt, pepper, and water, and simmer for 5 more minutes. Transfer the escarole to a baking dish.

5. Let the braising liquid reduce for about 1 minute over medium-high heat.

6. Sprinkle the escarole with the olives, capers, raisins, pignoli, and 1 tablespoon (7 g) grated cheese. Pour half of the braising liquid over the escarole. Cover the escarole with bread crumbs and the remaining 1 tablespoon (7 g) grated cheese. Pour the remaining braising liquid over the escarole and drizzle with olive oil.

7. Bake the escarole for 20 to 30 minutes, or until browned on top. Serve immediately.

iNDEX

iNDEX

iNDEX

ACKNOWLEDGMENTS

I thank God, Earth, and Mother Nature for the bounty provided to me for my "foodie" endeavors. It is a blessing to have access to fresh, wholesome, and natural foods to create the dishes in this cookbook.

Thank you to my family and friends for supporting my efforts to craft my product, Flavor Bombs™, and for encouraging me to write the *Cooking with Flavor Bombs* cookbook. My children, Veronica, Michael, and Thomas, have been my inspiration for cooking delicious, healthy foods, in an effort to set them on the path to "enlightened eating." My husband, Michael, has been my taste tester, my number-one fan, and my "Shark" for thirty-eight years. He has my everlasting love and appreciation. My parents, Pat and Jean Eboli, provided me with the culinary foundation of our Italian heritage and introduced me to the "finer things in life" at an early age. Thank you, Mom, for being an excellent cook and for teaching me how to bread the cutlets, my first job in the kitchen. Thanks, Dad, for teaching me how to eat a lobster when I was a child!

I offer my sincerest thanks to Jeannine Dillon and Erin Canning of Race Point Publishing. Jeannine, for guiding me with her professional expertise to challenge myself and find my voice with this book, and Erin, for her vital assistance in getting my message on paper. Working with them and creating this cookbook has been a dream come true.

ABOUT THE AUTHOR

Chef Giovannina "Gio" Bellino is a longtime "foodie" entrepreneur and the owner of Goddess Gourmet, a catering company on Long Island, New York. She launched her Flavor Bombs™ product line in 2015.

Flavor Bombs™ are manufactured in Yaphank, New York, at Ever So Saucy Foods, a state-of-the-art facility owned and operated by renowned chef Frank Tramontano. Flavor Bombs™ is a line of all-natural, fresh-frozen, gluten-free, low-sodium, and affordable recipe-ready cooking bases that enhance the flavor and cooking experience of everyday dishes. Flavor Bombs™ come in five exciting flavors, including Basil, Sage, Rosemary, Mirepoix, and Soffritto. Flavor Bombs™ are packed in 2-ounce (56 g) containers and were developed to provide consumers with a unique cooking base to create a memorable dish for four or more people. Flavor Bombs™ are now available in the United States for retail. For more information regarding Flavor Bombs™ contact Giovannina Bellino at (516) 369-7236 or e-mail her at gio@flavorbombs.net. Flavor Bombs™ are also available for purchase at flavorbombs.net.

My obsession with great taste and nutrition is what separates Flavor Bombs™ from everything within the cooking-base category. We use only fresh herbs and all-natural ingredients, and produce Flavor Bombs™ in small batches locking in their freshness. The concentration and layering of flavors and ingredients in Flavor Bombs™ allow for an "explosion" of flavors and aromas that turns everyday dishes into gourmet meals. Flavor Bombs™ are precooked so they are versatile enough to use to start *or* finish a dish.

Learn more about Gio at goddessgourmet.com and sexfoodrockandroll.com. Follow her on Twitter (@goddessgio), Instagram (flavor_bombs), and Facebook (Flavor Bombs).